P9-DDM-254

MY
GRANDFATHER'S
GALLERY

MY GRANDFATHER'S GALLERY

A FAMILY MEMOIR OF ART AND WAR

ANNE SINCLAIR

TRANSLATED FROM THE FRENCH BY SHAUN WHITESIDE

FARRAR, STRAUS AND GIROUX NEW YORK

Farrar, Straus and Giroux
18 West 18th Street, New York 10011

Owing to limitations of space, illustration credits appear on page 225.

Library of Congress Cataloging-in-Publication Data
Sinclair, Anne, author.
    [21, rue La Boétie. English]
    My grandfather's gallery : a family memoir of art and war / Anne
Sinclair ; translated by Shaun Whiteside.
        pages   cm
    ISBN 978-0-374-25162-8 (hardback) — ISBN 978-0-374-71179-5 (ebook)
    1. Sinclair, Anne—Family.   2. Rosenberg, Paul, 1881–1959.
3. Journalists—France—Biography.   4. Art dealers—France—
Biography.   I. Whiteside, Shaun, translator.   II. Title.

PN5183.S54 A313 2014
709.2—dc23
[B]
                                                              2014004038

Designed by Jonathan D. Lippincott

Farrar, Straus and Giroux books may be purchased for educational,
business, or promotional use. For information on bulk purchases,
please contact the Macmillan Corporate and Premium Sales
Department at 1-800-221-7945, extension 5442, or write to
specialmarkets@macmillan.com.

www.fsgbooks.com
www.twitter.com/fsgbooks • www.facebook.com/fsgbooks

10 9 8 7 6 5 4 3 2 1

Frontispiece: Drawing of Paul Rosenberg by Pablo Picasso,
winter 1918–1919

To my mother,
Micheline Rosenberg-Sinclair

CONTENTS

MY
GRANDFATHER'S
GALLERY

PROLOGUE

On June 10, 2013, seventy-four years after my grand-father was forced to abandon his gallery located at 21 rue La Boétie in Paris, I had the honor to unveil a white marble plaque on the façade of the building. The plaque bore his name and those of famous painters he used to show, many of whom were his closest friends—Picasso, Braque, Matisse, Léger among them. I was pleased that the plaque explained who my grandfather was and how the build-ing, which had been devoted for twenty years to art, had been looted and transformed into a Nazi propaganda office during the German occupation of France.

The initiative was not mine. Rather, the owner of the building, of whom I had never heard, a certain M. Thélot, a French "entrepreneur," who used to rent offices in the building, unexpectedly sent me a very moving letter. He had just been browsing in a bookshop and had seen a book whose title was the exact address of the building he owned. Curious, he bought the volume—the French edition of this book, *21, rue La Boétie*—and was so moved by the story that he offered to have a plaque made for the front of the building, as is commonly done for famous French or foreign citizens who have left their mark on a place. Moreover, he renamed the main room inside the gallery, the one where exhibitions had been held before the war, the Paul Rosenberg Room. (Previous tenants had improbably called it the Mississippi Room.) These initiatives were so selfless and elegant that I accepted with joy.

The homage took place on a late afternoon, when the sun was shining over Paris, so many years after the Nazis had seized the gallery.

I could imagine how proud my grandparents, my uncle, and my mother, all of them now dead, would have been had they known their home would become celebrated in Paris, nearly three-quarters of a century after they were forced to flee arrest and deportation because they were Jewish and had refused to collaborate with the Nazi government that deemed modern painting "degenerate art."

From now on, thanks to M. Thélot, everyone passing by will read the plaque, learn who the great art dealer Paul Rosenberg was, and discover how a criminal regime transformed my grandfather's gallery from a temple of beauty to a storeroom of depravity.

That is the story of this book.

INTRODUCTION

A day of rain and demonstrations, early 2010.

My neighborhood has been closed off by the police, the streets are jammed around the Bastille, and I am a prisoner in a car that I can't simply abandon in the middle of the road. At last, reaching a CRS (state police force) barrier blocking off the Boulevard Beaumarchais, near the Place de la Bastille, I wind down my window and ask the soaked cop if I can slip by like the other local residents. "Your papers," he says wearily. I've just moved in, and I haven't got a driver's license or any ID with my new address on it. He's sorry, he can't take my word for it. I need proof of my new place of residence. I can't get home.

—

A little while later I write to the office in Nantes that issues copies of birth certificates to French citizens born abroad. When it sends me the document, I go to the police station nearest to my house, quai de Gesvres, armed with the necessary papers: the birth certificate they have asked for as well as my recently renewed identity card, valid for another seven years.

A long queue. I take my ticket and wait for an hour and a half, long enough to look around at the people who have come to pick up IDs or passports and to hear the overworked clerks bluntly questioning the assembled supplicants. "Madame, I must know whether or not you are from Guadeloupe!" an old woman is asked in a tone that sounds a lot harsher than if she were asked, "Are you originally from the Loire-Atlantique?"

At last it's my turn. I take the papers out of my file. It is then that a man behind the counter is astonished to discover that I was born abroad. I tell him that since I was born in New York, my administrative papers had to come from the offices in Nantes. He then asks for my parents' birth certificates. I spare him their story: how they met after the war when my father had been demobilized from the Free French forces. I refrain from explaining that I was born in America by chance and stayed there for only two years before coming to France to spend the rest of my life here because my father couldn't find a job. I'm an inch away from trying to find excuses for being born outside French territory.

On the other hand, I am feeling a bit surprised by his insistence on asking for my parents' birth certificates. Besides, I add that on mine—look, monsieur—it clearly states that Anne S. is the daughter of Robert S. and Micheline R., both born in Paris, and that I'm therefore what's known as French by affiliation. I also hand him my identity card, issued three years ago and valid until 2017, which means that it's up to the administration to demonstrate that it is fraudulent, should it have any suspicion.

But he persists: the papers are necessary; there are new directives dating from 2009 for any citizen wishing to prove his "Frenchness."

"Are your four grandparents French?" asks the man behind the counter.

Fearing I may have misheard, I ask him to repeat the question.

"Your four grandparents, were they born in France, yes or no?"

"The last time people of their generation were asked this kind of question was before they were put on a train to Pithiviers or Beaune-la-Rolande!" I say, my voice choking with rage, as I name the French camps where Jews were locked up by the French collaborating police before being deported by the Nazis to the death camps.

"What? What train? What are you talking about? I must repeat that I need that document. Don't come back until you have it in your possession."

He dismisses me abruptly, pushing toward me my file, which by the purest coincidence is yellow, the very color of the star Jews had to wear on their clothes.

No point in giving a history lesson to a clerk to whom the Vichy laws mean nothing and to whom no one responsible for the new regulations has taken the time to explain that there are unfortunate turns of phrase, reminiscent of more troubled times, that might be best avoided.

I leave, more hurt than angry with this draconian desk clerk, feeling that my birth is somehow suspect, as if there were two categories of French people, some more

French than others. I'm also thinking about the absurdity of this situation, given that other officials, years ago, unaware of the doubts surrounding my origins, appointed me the model for their statue of Marianne, the symbol of France, worthy to take pride of place in their town halls.

This isn't just an administrative bore. It's the revival of an unhealthy debate about national identity that has been poisoning France in the last few years.

The incident calls to mind a memory from my youth. In the 1970s the Holocaust blew up in our faces, especially through discovery of the Vichy regime's involvement in the final solution. We might think of the famous interview in *L'Express* with Louis Darquier de Pellepoix, the general commissioner for Jewish questions, in which, from his exile in Spain, he stated without the slightest remorse that "only lice were gassed in Auschwitz." This was the starting point for the inquiries and investigations led by the lawyer and author Serge Klarsfeld* into crimes against humanity, chiefly directed—this was before the trial of Maurice Papon†—at René Bousquet, the general secretary of the Vichy police. It was a time when significant books on the subject were starting to be published, the first of them, *Vichy France and the Jews*, by the American historians Michael R. Marrus and Robert O. Paxton.

We had had to wait for the research at universities

---

*A French lawyer who, along with his wife, Beate, dedicated his life to deportees. The Klarsfelds were known as Nazi hunters.
†Maurice Papon was sentenced in 1998 for "complicity in crimes against humanity" for his actions between 1942 and 1944, when he was the official representative of Vichy in the prefecture of Gironde, and especially for deporting Jews.

abroad to bring to light the role of the Vichy administration in the arrest and deportation of the Jews of France. It was the start of a great outpouring about the "dark years" and, in a seemingly parallel universe, the emergence of the revisionists, like Robert Faurisson, who was convicted several times in France for "denial of crimes against humanity."

—

Twenty years before, my parents had—as they used to say in those days—"done up" an old farm in Seine-et-Marne, a hundred miles from Paris, that served as a weekend retreat. My father, who worked in the cosmetics industry, had been pleased to meet a colleague in the same village, Jean Leguay, who ran Gemey, now a company affiliated with the L'Oréal group.

Leguay and my father played golf at Fontainebleau from time to time. Leguay often came to our house for coffee, with his wife, Minouchette, who, when I was a girl, represented for me all the snobbery of the Sixteenth Arrondissement. She claimed, in this little village of three hundred souls, to have wanted to repaint her house in "Dior gray," a color that wasn't listed in the Valentine paint catalog, but whose name had a pretty ring for her. In short, while Minouchette might have been silly and vain, her husband was pleasant and intelligent. My father enjoyed his company, and as a child happy to go out with her dad, I often followed them as they walked the golf course. Leguay had the smooth pink face of people who sleep soundly at night. My mother, who was always concerned about my father's pallor, frequently mentioned Leguay as an example of someone exuding health and well-being, a man at ease with himself.

—

A few years before this national reexamination of the scale of collaboration in Vichy and the treatment of the Jews, Robert Laffont published a book by Claude Lévy and Paul Tillard titled *La Grande rafle du Vel d'Hiv*, about the massive July 1942 roundup at a Paris sports stadium where Jews were held in hideous conditions for weeks before being deported to Auschwitz. Nowadays that event is well known to the French, especially because of the speech delivered by Jacques Chirac on July 16, 1995, acknowledging France's culpability in the deportation of the Jews. Various books and a few films, including *La Rafle* (*The Roundup*), helped bring the story to public attention. But that hadn't yet happened in the late 1960s, when the publication of excerpts from Lévy and Tillard's book in the national press caused an uproar.

The excerpts concerned a certain Leguay, no first name given. The reader learned that Leguay had been the secretary-general of the Vichy police, René Bousquet's delegate in the Nazi-occupied zone of France. Since Leguay himself was a prefect, he was in constant correspondence with his colleagues about the practical problems posed by the arrest of the Jews. He also witnessed the roundups in July 1943, which he had helped organize, and directed the transfer of Jews from the *zone libre* to the Drancy internment camp.

Like Bousquet, who had long enjoyed the protection of his political friends, such as Maurice Papon, the only senior Vichy official to have been put on trial over the last twenty years, Jean Leguay was a disreputable character whose crimes remained unknown for a long time, thanks to countless collaborators whose pasts came to light only much later. Besides, at that time I would have laughed at anyone who had told me that some twenty-seven years later a book by Pierre Péan titled *Une Jeunesse française* (A French Youth) would reveal, with the consent of its chief protagonist, the dark years of the man who later became President François Mitterrand. At the Institut d'Études Politiques de Paris I had physically fought against the *majos*, the elite right-wing students who represented the majority of the school's students during the 1970s. Unlike us, the left-wing *minos*, these students maintained (rightly, alas) that Mitterrand had been awarded the Ordre de la Francisque, the highest honor given in Vichy France.

So Péan told this charged story about his old friends with murky pasts. But what startled me at the time wasn't so much the revelation of the dubious life of one François Mitterrand, who had served the Vichy regime before becoming François Morland and fighting with the Resistance, as the enduring nature of his dubious friendships, which he never denied. His links with René Bousquet, of course, confirmed by the president himself and attested to by photographs taken at Latche, Mitterrand's house in Les Landes in the southwest of France while he was financing his various political campaigns, were also alarming, as well as his closeness to Jean-Paul Martin, a former *cagoulard*—a member of the French fascist organization La Cagoule—for whose funeral, in 1986, Mitterrand, by then the president of the French Republic, had asked that the coffin be draped with the French flag.

To this day, I retain a sense of gratitude to former President Mitterrand for bringing the left back to power after twenty years and admiration for his tireless efforts on behalf of Europe. But by the time his past was discovered and even acknowledged by him, I had forever lost my faith in the sincerity of his moral and political commitments, and I was left with a powerful sense of betrayal. The indignation that I felt as my convictions about the past of the French nation were so cataclysmically overturned will never leave me.

For my father, the revelations about the Vel d'Hiv roundup were experienced as a searing pain, all the more excruciating for the fact that his own father, who had worn the yellow star before going into hiding under the name of Sabatier, had been denounced by the concierge of the building in which he had taken refuge with my grandmother. He had subsequently been arrested and interned in Drancy by the French police.

How could I fail, while bringing alive the story of my maternal family, to pay homage to my father's mother, Marguerite Schwartz?* In a wildly novelistic scene that I have never fully understood, she managed, thanks to a

---

*Translator's note: Both of Anne's grandmothers were named Marguerite. For clarity, Anne's paternal grandmother is referred to here and throughout as Marguerite, while her maternal grandmother is called by her family nickname, Margot.

French officer with contacts in Drancy, to disguise herself as a nurse, borrow a Red Cross ambulance and some false papers, and get my paternal grandfather out of that antechamber to deportation. His health ruined by the long period of mistreatment he had undergone, he died just one year later—but in his bed, rather than in the Auschwitz gas chamber, where the next convoy would have taken him.

—

My father, that day in 1967, had difficulty believing that the official who had taken an active role in those deportation-related activities was the same Leguay with whom, the previous weekend, he had shared a friendly cup of tea.

Armed with a photocopy of a letter from the Leguay in question, addressed to the Germans and found at the Center of Contemporary Jewish Documentation (CDSE; now part of the Shoah Memorial in Paris), my father went to the headquarters of the French Society of Perfumers and asked the chairman to show him a business letter signed by Jean Leguay, the president of Gemey. As he reviewed this document, my father turned very pale: the two signatures were identical. My father then told the chairman what he knew about this character and demanded that he be thrown out of the association. He was met with embarrassed refusal on the part of the chairman. It was not very courageous, and the times were not yet attuned to these injustices, the French lagging well behind the Germans in their desire to achieve transparency about their past. In those years the desire not to "create a scandal" outweighed all other considerations.

After resigning from the professional association, my father wrote to Leguay to tell him what he knew about his past and asked him to walk on the other side of the road in their village, so that he would never run into him again. Leguay responded by sending my father the ruling by the High Court of Justice that had cleared him in 1949, as it had Bousquet and many others.

On a side note, during those years, Gemey was bought by L'Oréal, a company known for its recycling of notorious collaborators. These included Jean Filliol, who had tried to assassinate the Jewish French prime minister Léon Blum before the war and who had, after the liberation, taken refuge in Spain, where he ran the Spanish branch of L'Oréal. Filliol had been sentenced to death in absentia for having been a member of Joseph Darnand's militia and for facilitating the horrific Nazi revenge attack on the town of Oradour in 1944. Another senior executive with L'Oréal, Jacques Corrèze, coincidentally lived in the same building as Jean Leguay in Paris at rue de Rémusat, and had been an officer in Eugène Deloncle's fascist Cagoule organization, which was financed by Eugène Schueller, the father of Liliane Bettencourt, the wealthy socialite and major shareholder of L'Oréal.

In 1941, Jacques Corrèze joined the Legion of French Volunteers (LVF) against Bolshevism, which fought alongside the Charlemagne Regiment, the Waffen-SS division that included Frenchmen who had decided to fight in the Waffen-SS uniform. Sentenced to ten years' imprisonment in 1948, he was freed a year later and was immediately hired by Schueller to become the chief executive of L'Oréal in America. Amnestied in 1959 and rehabilitated in the

1960s, he died in Paris in 1991, while the American Office of Special Investigations was investigating his possible involvement in crimes committed during the war.

The recent Bettencourt affair,* which has nothing to do with the above, did recall Schueller's past and put these episodes from the history of the founder of L'Oréal in the spotlight once more.

—

The dossier painstakingly compiled by Serge Klarsfeld enabled the justice system to find Jean Leguay guilty of crimes against humanity. I remember taking my father along to the press conference at which Klarsfeld argued that the legal proceedings to charge Bousquet and Leguay with crimes against humanity were fully justified. This was in 1979. My father told me, as he left Klarsfeld's office, "You'll see, he'll die after me, peacefully, in his sleep." Indeed, my father, who was the same age as Leguay, died the next year, while Leguay died in 1989, but before his trial could begin. According to the ruling that stated that legal action had been abandoned, "there was information to establish that he had taken part in crimes against humanity."

—

My mishap at the police station was pretty harmless in the scheme of things, but the questioning of my identity brought a tidal wave of family memories surging forward.

---

*Translator's note: The Bettencourt affair was a 2010 French political scandal that erupted over Liliane Bettencourt's illegal political campaign donations to members of the French government associated with Nicolas Sarkozy.

For years I had refused to listen to the stories of the past told over and over again by my mother. Not out of a desire to reject my family, but the story of my maternal grandparents, even though I thought I knew it, never felt as if it belonged to me, as if it related to my life. It even bored me a bit. What I liked was politics, journalism; my father's world rather than my mother's. My father, who had joined the Free French in the Middle East during the war; my father, who, under the name of Jacques Breton, had delivered editorials on Radio Beirut on behalf of General Charles de Gaulle; my father, so proud to show me the agency dispatch in which Joseph Goebbels had condemned him to death and railed against "the Jew Sinclair"; my father, having returned to Paris after the liberation, paying a final visit to his own father, who had been seriously ill since Drancy. Even though my father himself built an industrial career as a business executive far from my own areas of interest, I felt closer to the war stories he recorded in his notebooks than I did to my mother's side of the family, which lived under the shadow of my art dealer grandfather, who had died when I was only eleven years old. In short, I secretly felt I was on the same side as "My Father the Hero," who gently mocked "My Mother Who Sat Out the War on Fifth Avenue."

My father, Robert Sinclair, who was called Robert Schwartz throughout his youth, was sent to the front in 1939 as a thirty-year-old soldier, on meteorological duty. He was stationed at a border post (might it have been the Maginot Line?) and played chess, one move per day with a colleague who had been sent to a different strategic location, taking advantage of their daily call to compare weather conditions on the front. They sat there and waited for the enemy, who never came because they had decided to avoid that predictable line of defense. (I like to imagine him moving his rook or his knight, occasionally sticking his hand outside and saying, "It's raining," to his friend, who would reply, "Here too!") When he was finally demobilized, he returned to Paris and, like many others, wept at the sight of flags bearing the swastika fluttering over the Champs-Élysées. He remembered the day he had stood there with his mother, on November 11, 1918, applauding Marshal Ferdinand Foch's troops as they celebrated the victory of the First World War. He was just a nine-year-old boy, but he told me he knew that he was destined to enlist from that time.

Unaware of the networks that would have enabled him to pass through England, he managed to reach the United States via a series of complicated routes, and it was there that he enrolled in Free France, which ultimately sent him to Damascus, Beirut, and Cairo. Before boarding the ship bound for the Middle East via the Atlantic and the Indian Ocean, all lights extinguished so as not to alert the enemy, he was told that the Germans were aware of the surnames of French officers who had enlisted with de Gaulle and whose families had stayed in France. To protect his relatives, he was compelled to change his name. Wanting to retain his initials, he opened the New York City phone book to the letter *S* and stumbled upon the name Sinclair, perhaps no more unusual in the United States than Martin or Dupont in France.

I have always been a bit irritated with him for wanting to keep the name Sinclair and then legally adopting it as his surname after the war. It meant losing a part of our identity. But he had earned a name for himself under that nom de guerre; he bore it proudly and probably wanted to allow his descendants—me, as it happened—to avoid the dangers that a Jewish name had inflicted on his family. This was not unusual among those traumatized by the war in the years that followed the liberation, but I confess that I've always experienced it as a sort of denial. That's probably why I laid claim to my Jewish identity very early on. And why I've been distressed by those who, playing with proportional representation, allowed the extreme-right Front National (FN) to exist politically in France. It's why I fought bitterly against the media access so generously granted to the FN in the 1980s and why for ten years I refused to have Jean-Marie Le Pen on my television program, *7 sur 7*, which was a discussion of the previous week's political news. The pointlessness of this battle became apparent on April 21, 2002, and in the years that followed, when Le Pen came in second in the general election, the consequences of which we are still living with today.

So much for rummaging around in the cardboard boxes of family archives. As I went through all those random papers, I eventually came across my original birth certificate, rather than the copy generally required by the administrative services. What would the clerk at the prefecture, who prompted this book, after all, have said if he had seen that I had been born Anne Schwartz, *dite* Sinclair, and that my name was only officially changed in 1949, when I was one year old?

—

In my youth I was more receptive to the story of my paternal grandparents, who had stayed in France, than I was to the fate of those who, pursued by the Nazis, had managed to flee and were then dispossessed, plundered, and stripped of their nationality. Besides, I wanted to build my own life, preferring television to art galleries, the public life to the artistic one, old newspapers to old paintings.

In 2006 my mother passed away. And as always after the death of a parent, you're struck by all the things you've neglected to ask or didn't want to know, whether out of laziness or weariness at hearing the same stories again and again. In my mother's flat, I emptied cupboards crammed with dusty memories: old keys, outmoded furs, family photographs, and stacks of papers that had accumulated over the course of decades.

Then I turned sixty and happened to spend a few years in the United States, a country that constantly brought me back to my childhood and to the part of the family that had sought refuge there. And here were the French authorities, playing with dangerous ideas, reminding me that French nationality can't be taken for granted even if you've had it all your life. How fragile it is to those who bear it and how inaccessible to those who wish to lay claim to it. And reminding me that it wasn't the first time this had happened in my family.

I realized I hadn't even had time to unpack the boxes from my mother's apartment, which I'd stacked in a closet. They were full of letters and old files that I'd picked up without even giving them a thought. Suddenly unable to contain my curiosity, I plunged into the family archives, in search of the story of my past. To find out who my mother's father really was: my grandfather Paul Rosenberg, a man hailed as a pioneer in the world of painting, of modern art, who then became a pariah in his own country during the Second World War. I yearned to fit together the pieces of this French story of art and war.

I am the granddaughter of Paul Rosenberg, a gentleman who lived in Paris and who owned a gallery at 21 rue La Boétie.

RUE LA BOÉTIE

Number 21. I've passed by it hundreds of times. My mother liked to show me the 1930s façade with its stone arches. I'd noticed various shops on that street—ice cream, pizza—but I'd never stopped to take a closer look. Now, seventy years after my grandfather had left the premises, I wanted to see the building for myself. I couldn't imagine that three years later I would unveil a plaque on this very building that I had not yet entered.

Today it's an office of the Veolia Environmental Services company. I call them up: "My grandparents used to live there. I'd love to take a look around, really just a look. I don't want to disturb you . . . It was before the war, I'm sure there are few traces left . . . Of course I understand if it's not possible." I detected the ambivalence in my own voice. It was almost as if I worried that they might actually let me in.

They did. Why would they resist? So one Wednesday in April 2010 off I went to Veolia, to 21 rue La Boétie, where I begin my story. Touched by my curiosity and possibly a bit incredulous that it's taken me to the age of sixty to set foot in the building where my grandfather's gallery was located, my hosts graciously show me around.

The hallway has been divided, and there are white stucco columns with Corinthian capitals, which I find a bit tasteless. Are they original? And a black-and-white damier marble floor. It's all been redesigned, modernized, the rooms, the spaces. There are spotlights affixed to the ceiling. The staircase with its old-fashioned banisters leading to the upper floors seems unchanged. Lots of Fernand Léger's and André Masson's paintings used to hang on the walls of this interior stairway, which led to my family's private apartments: the one belonging to my grandparents and their children, then the one to my great-grandmother, Paul's mother, Mathilde Rosenberg. Of course no paintings now hang in this stairway, which leads to various offices. The overall impression is dreary. Yet the elevator is modern, surely in compliance with health and safety regulations. The rattling old cage of another age is gone.

The stairway within the gallery, the one with the cast-iron banister, seems to have retained its original look, from the 1930s, when my grandfather did some elaborate renovations. The floor is patterned with marble mosaics made with yellow stones. But there's no way of telling exactly where the mosaic plaques went, the ones designed by Georges Braque, who also supervised their installation. Above the stairs were arches, replicas of the ones outside, adorned with pieces of mirrored glass.

I'm in the lower of the two exhibition halls, the one that appears in so many of the photographs I've seen of my grandfather situated in his domain. All the exhibitions at rue La Boétie were held in this large room. A month of Braque, another of Henri Matisse, a third of Pablo Picasso. It is now a boardroom for Veolia executives. The fine oak parquet floor is still there, and I immediately recognize the wood paneling, which I've seen in the photographs, as well as the glass ceiling with its little star-shaped windows, which, as in other galleries of the time, diffused the light so as to soften the hard edges of cubist painting.

If I half closed my eyes I could see them, those big paintings from the 1920s and 1930s, hanging on the walls. Soon after, those masterpieces would be replaced by portraits of the head of the Vichy government, Marshal Philippe Pétain.

In 1927 E. Tériade, a famous critic and art publisher of Greek descent, described the Galerie Rosenberg in "Feuilles volantes," the monthly supplement of the influential journal *Cahiers d'art*: "We are introduced into a huge room, high-ceilinged, bare walls, naked light, a room in which sober brown curtains weigh down on the collection, in which two solitary armchairs upholstered with dark velvet reach toward you like two grand inquisitors; no, they're not reaching toward you, they're going for your throat, as masterpieces do. Hurricanes of solitude, of austerity, pass through the room . . . Paul Rosenberg: he's dressed in black. He has the anxious face of an ascetic or a passionate businessman."[1]

Here's another description of the setting, particularly interesting when you consider that the author is the notorious, extreme-right-wing writer Maurice Sachs, who later defined himself as a Jew, a homosexual, and a collaborator before being killed by a bullet to the back of the head by the Germans in whose service he had worked: "His grand seigneur bearing was part of his particular genius . . . You step into Rosenberg's gallery as if entering a temple: the deep leather armchairs, the walls lined with red silk, would lead you to think you were in a fine museum . . . He knew how to cast an extraordinary light on the painters he took under his wing. His knowledge of painting was deeper than that of his colleagues, and he had a very sure sense of his own taste."[2]

Paul, who had taken over his father's gallery with his brother, Léonce, in 1905, decided to set up on his own in 1910 and moved alone to 21 rue La Boétie, in the Eighth Arrondissement of Paris. Nineteenth-century works were shown on the mezzanine; contemporary art, on the ground floor. If visitors were unsure about Braque or Léger, Paul invited them upstairs to see softer-contoured works by Edgar Degas, Pierre-Auguste Renoir, or Auguste Rodin. He hoped they might buy some of these, which would allow him to support his unknown friends, such as Picasso or Marie Laurencin, the muse of the poet Guillaume Apollinaire. In 1913 she became the first artist to sign an exclusive deal with Paul, an arrangement that stood until 1940. She was joined by Picasso in 1918, Braque in 1923, Léger in 1926, and Matisse in 1936.

—

In 1912, almost as soon as he had moved in, Paul sent out an announcement just as anyone opening a shop might do, describing his new venture: "I will shortly be opening new modern art galleries at 21 rue La Boétie, where I plan to hold periodic exhibitions by the masters of the nineteenth century and painters of our own times. In my view, however, the shortcoming of contemporary exhibitions is that they show an artist's work in isolation. So I intend to hold group exhibitions of decorative art . . . Not only do I plan to offer my spaces for free, I shall not take a percentage in the event of a sale. For each exhibition I shall publish at my own expense a catalog of the paintings, sculptures, furniture, etc."

The critic Pierre Nahon stresses Paul's desire to establish a connection between French painting of the past and the modernist trends of the twentieth century, noting that in the late 1930s Paul had on his walls and in his inventory a collection of Géricault, Ingres, Delacroix, Courbet, Cézanne, Manet, Degas, Monet, Renoir, Gauguin, Toulouse-Lautrec, Picasso, Braque, Léger, Le Douanier Rousseau, Bonnard, Laurencin, Modigliani, and Matisse. "The gallery," Nahon writes, "is becoming an essential meeting place for everyone who wants to follow the development and the work of the innovative painters."

My own research is centered on an attempt to conjure the grandfather I barely knew. And to summon up the *riches heures* of the thirties and the grim ones of the forties that are integral to his story.

—

My grandfather had great difficulty regaining possession of his gallery after the war. The state had confiscated the building from the collaborators in August 1944 and made it the headquarters of the Saint-Gobain construction company, before finally returning the building to my grandfather. By then it had endured the sinister events that I am about to relate, events with which my grandfather could never make peace. Paul finally sold 21 rue La Boetie in January 1953. He was determined never again to live in that place, its basement filled with propaganda from the darkest years, its rooms still haunted by the ghosts of the occupation.

For a long time the building was home to the French General Information Service, Renseignements Généraux, the French police intelligence service, and the secrets of the Republic were buried with the secrets of the collaborators.

NUMBER 21 UNDER
THE GERMANS

21 rue La Boétie was piled to the rafters with those "accursed" or decadent works, the kind that the Nazis called *entartete Kunst* (EK), "degenerate art." The term referred to any art that, for the new German regime, departed from the canon of what the Nazis considered traditional.

"German people, come and judge for yourselves," said Adolf Ziegler, the president of the Reich Chamber of Visual Arts, as he infamously opened the Munich exhibition of degenerate art on July 18, 1937.[1]

This vast exhibition of six thousand works, taken from every museum in Germany, was hastily assembled. The intention was to ridicule modern art before imposing a ban on its sale. These works were deliberately shown among drawings by children or the mentally handicapped: there were two adjacent halls, with official German art hung in the first and the art identified as "degenerate" (Picasso, Braque, Matisse, Léger, Miró, Masson, Dalí, Chagall) exhibited in the second. Many of the works shown in the second hall had been confiscated from museums or private galleries mainly managed by Jews. Some were intentionally destroyed, while others were auctioned off for the benefit of the Nazi regime. Ironically, this attempt to ridicule modern art was to the great advantage of art lovers throughout the world. Vincent van Gogh quickly became the bestselling "degenerate" painter on the market. By the time the Reich Chamber exhibition closed on November 30, 1937, it had drawn more than two million viewers.

—

Joseph Goebbels, the propaganda minister, had planned the show as a counterpoint to the *Great Exhibition of German Art*, which opened simultaneously in Munich. It celebrated female farmers and soldiers, brave mothers, and rural landscapes of Greater Germany. In Goebbels's words, a distinction had to be made between "the art of those days and the art of these days."[2] He felt that German museums had to be cleansed of works produced after 1910.

The German rejection of novelty in art was nothing new. As Lynn H. Nicholas explains in her remarkable book *The Rape of Europa*, the antimodern tradition had a long history, "reaching back to Kaiser Wilhelm's 1909 firing of Hugo von Tschudi, director of the Nationalgalerie, for buying Impressionist paintings."[3] In 1893 a very influential book was published by the Jewish social critic Max Nordau, who first used the word *Entartung*, "degeneracy," to refer to artistic disciplines. In his most famous book, *Degeneration*, Nordau describes modern art as symptomatic of the degeneracy of society at the end of the nineteenth century. He declares all modern art, including that of the impressionists, "pathological." Nordau was both a Zionist and a Dreyfusard and a man developing conservative ideas about the founding principles of German culture. In the 1920s a group of philosophers put forward the concept of "degenerate art" on the basis of Nordau's work, at the risk of somewhat misrepresenting his ideas.[4]

After Hitler came to power in 1933, many artists chose to go into exile. Not only could they no longer show their work or sell it, they were forbidden to buy brushes, canvases, or paint. "The smell of turpentine in the air or a container of wet brushes was grounds for arrest," writes Nicholas.[5]

On June 30, 1939, just weeks before the outbreak of war, the Germans held a massive auction in Lucerne, featuring 126 paintings and sculptures from the most important museums and private collections in Germany. Many collectors, unable to resist the temptation to buy outstanding works of art at low prices, attended. Paul warned potential buyers that any currency the Reich harvested from this sale "would fall back on our heads in the form of bombs." Alfred Barr, the director of the prestigious Museum of Modern Art in New York, also tried to alert those museums that had announced their intention to buy. But to no avail. "Acceptance of these warnings was not made easier by the very mixed reception all modern art had endured for many years," writes Nicholas.[6]

From that moment Karl Haberstock, the Nazis' chief

art buyer, became one of the Führer's personal dealers. As Haberstock began to amass a collection of old masters for Hitler, he found intermediaries in France through whom he could purge all modernist impurities. Among them was the author and Nazi apologist Lucien Rebatet, who proposed the "Aryanization" of our fine arts.

There was a great deal of debate on this subject among Nazi officials, in particular between Goebbels and Alfred Rosenberg (Hitler's ideological theorist, who later was placed in charge of the "occupied Eastern territories"—in other words, the massacres that took place there). This unfortunate namesake of Paul's considered any form of physical distortion on a canvas "degenerate art," while Goebbels believed that modern painting could become part of a National Socialist revolutionary art movement. As in any totalitarian regime claiming to define a "new man" and a new world order, art was a priority for the apostles of National Socialism. Indeed, the Nazis were obsessed with the idea of turning art into an instrument of propaganda. In her book *L'Art de la défaite* (*Art of the Defeat*), Laurence Bertrand Dorléac relates how, several days after the armistice between Germany and the French Third Republic, the looting of artworks began on a massive scale. In fact, on June 30, 1940, Hitler issued an order to put artworks belonging to Jews in "safe-keeping." The term was chosen deliberately as a cover for what could only be described as theft. It was then that Alfred Rosenberg set up the Einsatzstab Reichsleiter Rosenberg (ERR). This became the chief organization in the Nazi looting operation, which put its stamp of infamy on all works of art confiscated by the occupying troops.

—

From early July 1940, Rosenberg instructed the army to raid the big Parisian art dealers and seize their collections. This represented the triumph of the Rosenberg-Göring clan over the tribe based around Joachim von Ribbentrop, the Reich foreign minister, and Otto Abetz, Hitler's ambassador to Paris during the Second World War. And as we know, Göring was immoderate about helping himself.[7]

From October 1940, organized theft followed upon random robbery. "The artworks were first assembled at the Musée du Jeu de Paume and the Louvre, then photographed, valued, recorded, and wrapped ready for transport to Germany," writes Dorléac.[8] Naturally, this contraband included both the classical paintings from the Parisian galleries and modern works, which, as Dorléac puts it, served as "bargaining chips for pieces more in line with the Nazi aesthetic."

—

In her classic account, *Le Front de l'art*, Rose Valland, the heroic protector of French artworks, relates that at the height of the war in 1943 she witnessed a column of smoke rising from the terrace of the Tuileries; it rose from paintings stamped with the letters *EK* (*entartete Kunst*), and signed Masson, Miró, Klee, Ernst, Léger, Picasso. "The men of the ERR planned to attack these paintings, run them through with swords, slash them with knives, and carry them to the pyre, as in those gigantic autos-da-fé that had taken place in the German museums, in a bid to destroy those works identified as 'degenerate.'"[9]

Valland was one of two people who tried to keep works of art from museums or private collections from being scattered across Germany. In this saga of art saved from the Nazi madness, the other hero working in the shadows was Jacques Jaujard, the director of the National Museums at the time, and the director of the Musée des Beaux-Arts after the war. It was he who suggested that the Germans draw up an inventory under Valland's direction. In *Le Front de l'art*, she tells how she managed to remain in her post at risk of her life in order to create a precise inventory of the stolen paintings. Rising to the post of captain in the French Army, she was sent to occupied Germany after the war to help France recover its stolen property.

This property came into consideration in the Nuremberg trials. Certainly, compared with the atrocities perpetrated upon human beings, the looting of art in Nazi-occupied territory seemed negligible. Still, the court considered it a war crime, on the ground that by attacking a culture, the Nazis were trying to destroy a people.

—

Consistent with their plan, as soon as the Nazis occupied Paris on June 14, 1940, they made their way to 21 rue La Boétie. But they were disappointed not to find the family patiently awaiting their arrival.

On July 4, 1940, the Reich ambassador, Otto Abetz, demanded that the building on rue La Boétie be sequestered by the police and that the artworks be seized. He had in fact just drawn up a list of Jewish dealers or collectors for the Gestapo: Bernheim-Jeune, Alphonse Kann, Jacques Seligmann, Wildenstein, and Paul Rosenberg.

This outrage continued with the German requisition of rue La Boétie in May 1941. On the eleventh day of that month, the brand-new Institut d'Étude des Questions Juives (IEQJ, Institute for the Study of Jewish Questions), was installed in the building with great pomp.

I've examined the few existing pictures of that installation, and more particularly, I've listened to Radio Paris on tapes supplied by the National Sound and Video Archives. The quality of the recording is excellent, with the nasal voice and wounding words of the speaker unmistakably clear: "Today saw the rechristening of the building previously occupied by Rosenberg; the name alone tells you all you need to know."

The ceremony opens with remarks on the "disastrous moral influence of Judaism," delivered by Clément Serpeille de Gobineau, a descendant of the more famous Arthur Comte de Gobineau, the author of the 1853 *An Essay on the Inequality of the Human Races.*

In the photographs and in the National Sound and Video Archives, you can see Louis-Ferdinand Céline, a star guest with impeccable far-right credentials, parking his bike in front of my grandfather's gallery, on which the name of that formidable new office stands out in capital letters. The porch and the famous exhibition hall are easily recognizable. A huge panel on the wall shows a woman on the ground covered with a French flag, a vulture perched on her belly, with the caption "Frenchmen, help me!"

In the exact place where my grandfather had hung paintings by Renoir, Picasso, and Léger over the previous few years, a tricolor flag, a portrait of Marshal Pétain, and quotations from Édouard Drumont, the author of *La France juive*, who, according to commentary of the time, "first raised the issue of the Jewish problem in all its magnitude": "The Jews came poor to a rich country. They are now the only rich people in a poor country." And that other quote on the opposite wall: "We are fighting the Jews to give France back its true, its familiar face."[10]

Capt. Paul Sézille was soon appointed secretary-general of the institute, a post he held until December 1942. He was a former right-hand man of the anti-Semitic activist and far-right politician Louis Darquier de Pellepoix and his prewar Anti-Jewish Union. A retired officer of the Foreign Legion, Sézille was, according to the historian Laurent Joly, a man drowning in booze and vitriol. "He was considered one of the most grotesque figures in anti-Semitism between 1940 and 1944, trying to give voice to a healthy France as it seeks to regain its true soul," writes Joly. [11]

He was followed shortly afterward, in January 1943, by the physician, anthropologist, and racial theorist George Montandon, who remained in office until the last days of August 1944, just before the liberation of Paris. The institute then assumed the name Institut d'Étude des

Questions Juives et Ethno-Raciales (IEQJER, Institute for the Study of Jewish and Ethno-Racial Questions). From that date, the Germans wanted to make the institute appear to be what we would now call a research center with the creation of six educational courses, including "Ethnoraciology," taught by Montandon himself, "Eugenics and Demographics," and "Judeocracy."

—

From the outset, the Institute for the Study of Jewish Questions, established in my family house, was an association created in accordance with the French Associations Law of 1901 and was devoted to anti-Semitic propaganda. Founded in May 1941, and cofinanced by the German Embassy and the Gestapo, it was not dependent on the Commissariat Général aux Questions Juives (set up by the Vichy government and run first by Xavier Vallat, then by Darquier de Pellepoix) but was in a direct line of command from the office of Otto Abetz. It was also controlled by "specialists" from Germany, including a certain Dr. Schwarz, a representative of an anti-Jewish institute in Frankfurt.

—

The IEQJ was in fact directed by Theodor Dannecker, the head of the Jewish Section (Judenreferat) of the Gestapo. Apparently, he had little confidence in the Vichy administration and wanted to set up—under the cover of a seemingly French organization effectively run by the Nazi services—an organization of anti-Semitic propagandists answerable to him alone. According to Joseph Billig, in his three-volume work devoted to the General Commissariat for Jewish Questions, "The 'final solution of the Jewish question' was from the very start in the hands of Dannecker's Judenreferat. The Judenreferat considered that it had been promised 'supreme power' over the Jews in France in the future . . . It was not primarily concerned with Jewish property. Its focus was the Jewish masses themselves. While awaiting the deportations, it organized the Jews into ghettos and prepared the raids."[12]

—

Secretary-General Sézille—was he sitting at Paul's desk?— took his orders only from Dannecker, whom he called, in the German style, "*mein Leutnant.*" He often asked the Propagandastaffel to support his private militia. He denounced "the spirit of indecision and the inadequate application of the [German] orders by the Commissariat for Jewish Questions." And he had no qualms about writing to Dannecker to thank him for the order requiring all Jews to wear the yellow star.

Though it was an organization under Nazi supervision, Sézille nevertheless sent the press a communiqué on August 21, 1941, affirming that the IEQJ "is an eminently French association, in accordance with the law of July 1, 1901, consisting of resolutely anti-Jewish men of good will . . . determined to resolve, at all cost and by all means, the Jewish question in France."

The institute's mission was to spread propaganda, and to collect letters of denunciation and ensure that they were "followed up." In a letter of January 31, 1942, addressed to Xavier Vallat, Sézille boasted of having thirty-three thousand members and seventy thousand signatures in his visitors' book. The institute published its journals, *Le Cahier jaune* and *La Question juive en France et dans le monde* (The Jewish Question in France and the World), and it put on its pièce de résistance, the exhibition *The Jew and France* at the Palais Berlitz in 1941. Otto Abetz later claimed that it had been organized by the Nazis themselves, but under the cover of the IEQJ for the benefit of the public. Which is to say that the offices at 21 rue La Boétie were working full tilt to organize the exhibition in time.

I went along to 30 boulevard des Italiens, to the Palais Berlitz, to see what remained of that space. But the walls are silent now. They've been replaced by the chain Bistro Romain and a multiplex cinema.

The cover of the September 6, 1941, issue of *L'Illustration* is well known. It reproduces the official poster of the exhibition, described by the magazine as a "large allegorical composition showing a kind of long-bearded vampire with thick lips and a hooked nose, with bony fingers like the claws of a bird of prey clutching a globe."[13]

In the cinemas, audiences watched news reports devoted to the famous exhibition.* The commentary accompanying the pictures is, like everything else, difficult to listen to, even more so sixty years on: "Out of every

---

*Marcel Ophuls, in his film *The Sorrow and the Pity*, shows pictures of the exhibition that always haunted me, even before I knew that it was at 21 rue La Boétie that the show had been conceived.

one hundred Frenchmen of old stock, ninety are true whites pure of any other racial mixture. The same cannot be said of the Jews. They are the product of racial mixing that occurred several millennia ago, between Aryans, Mongols, and Negroes. Consequently the Jew has his very own attitudes, gestures, and physiognomy. It is comforting to see the French going to see this exhibition. Henceforth they will be able to identify the Jew and protect themselves against his actions."

In this terrifying exhibition, life-size portraits, in black and white, are arranged like targets at a shooting gallery, with a picture of the former prime minister Léon Blum at the center. Below each portrait is the individual's name with a ribbon identifying his nationality followed by a question mark—"French?"—and the invariable exclamation "No, Jewish!"[14]

Some five hundred thousand tickets to the exhibition were sold. Counting half-price entrants, there were a million visitors in Paris before it traveled to other French cities, including, for a time, Bordeaux, Nancy, Marseille, Nice, Cannes, Toulouse, and Lyon, meaning that it also went to the unoccupied zone. History tells us little about whether people came out feeling informed and convinced or indignant and repelled.

—

Various odd characters anonymously frequented the offices at 21 rue La Boétie. Others, more famous, sometimes complained that they hadn't been treated very well. On October 21, 1941, Sézille received a letter of rebuke from Céline, who was "a little hurt not to see in the book-shop [of the exhibition] either one of his recent books: *Bagatelles [pour un massacre]* or *L'École [des cadavres]*,* while there was a flurry of insignificant little books . . . I observe once again the lamentable shortage (so sensitive in this case) of intelligence and Aryan solidarity." Sézille replied three days later: "I am myself terribly sorry not to have been able, in spite of all our requests of the publishers, to acquire the books of which you speak and which, I know, are ideally suited to wage the anti-Jewish struggle. But I wish to inform you that we have already had for sale in our shops large numbers of *Beaux draps* and *Mea culpa* [two other anti-Semitic tracts by Céline], and that these two books continue to be requested on a daily basis. Please believe me when I say that we have always done and will continue to do the impossible to distribute your works and make sure they have their rightful place."[15]

Who was this man, Capt. Paul Sézille, who was lucky enough to die on April 20, 1944, four months before the liberation of Paris? What hatred inspired him, what blindness afflicted him, what bitterness had he suffered to run this vile organization and publish his shameful books? After the liberation, my grandparents were stunned to discover whole cases of books published by the institute in the cellar of the building. Unfortunately, the notion of "bearing witness," of the "obligation to remember," that spread through France in the 1990s had not yet taken hold,

---

*Translator's note: *Bagatelles pour un massacre* and *L'École des cadavres* were two rabidly anti-Semitic pamphlets written by the respected novelist.

and my grandparents, rather than keep the archives, got rid of that library of shame at the first opportunity.

I kept for a long time the sole survivor of this collection, a book by Captain Sézille himself, whose oeuvre once filled the basement of rue La Boétie. And then, through the various comings and goings of the Rosenberg and Sinclair families, this literature and the trail of the sinister captain disappeared.

—

During the refurbishment of his gallery, which took several years and wasn't completed until 1934, Paul asked Picasso to make some marble patterns to be inlaid into the tile floor. Giving him lots of sketches in the hopes that Picasso would create something unique, he first asked him for his designs in August 1928. But since Picasso never met deadlines and took a lot of persuading to carry out any commission, Paul ended up commissioning Braque to complete the project. In each of the four corners of the gallery, Braque created a rectangular marble mosaic, faithfully scaled-down copies of four of his large still lifes: pitchers, plates, lemons, cutlery, and tablecloths well known in his paintings. It was no longer the cubist period—gray, green, and brown—when Braque and Picasso were painting similar pictures with the eternal guitar and the front page of *Le Journal*. So similar that partly out of a spirit of mischief and partly because they themselves no longer knew who had painted what, the paintings were signed arbitrarily.

The still lifes in question on the floor of my grandfather's gallery were brighter, more colorful, and more luminous than the works of that period. They lent themselves to mosaic treatment, recalling the designs on the floors of the patrician Roman villas in Pompeii or Volubilis.

After the war, when Paul sold the building he no longer wanted to live in, he had Braque's four marble mosaics cut out of the floor and made into low tables, framed in black marble. I lived alongside two of those tables throughout my youth and often stroked the marble, unaware of the innocent people, denounced and arrested, who had stepped upon them before being handed over to their executioners. The family house on rue La Boétie would have sheltered the executioners. I have never been able to watch Henri-Georges Clouzot's masterpiece *The Murderer Lives at Number 21*, without thinking about this.

FLOIRAC

From the earliest days of Nazism, Paul rejected the regime with every fiber of his being. He actively opposed the sale by the German government of "degenerate art." And as the president of the SNA, the French association of dealers in fine art and antiques, he tried to persuade his colleagues across Europe to boycott the sales. Yet few people resisted the often exceptional paintings cast onto the market in this way. But Paul would not relent. "Not a cent to the German Reich" was the slogan for a small group that saw masterpieces acquired by less scrupulous dealers disappearing before their eyes.

The Germans didn't forget Paul Rosenberg. In fact, they blacklisted him.

He had thwarted them to some extent, sending a number of works to safety in London and New York and lending others to American museums, notably to the Museum of Modern Art for the first big Picasso retrospective, which my grandfather himself had put together during several months in New York with his friend Alfred

Barr in 1939. Not surprisingly, in August of that year, my grandfather wrote to Picasso from Évian speaking of "dark events" as an inevitability.

—

On September 3, 1939, the day war is declared, my grandfather is with his family in the Touraine, near the Loire River, at Cinq-Mars-la-Pile. He closes his gallery and, for fear of bombing raids, takes some of his paintings to Tours. There he stores them under the name of his chauffeur, Louis Le Gall. These would be the first paintings recovered after the war because neither the Nazis nor the French authorities were aware of their existence.

Then the whole family leaves for Bordeaux, where, on February 7, 1940, they rent a house, Le Castel, at 12 Route de la Tresne, in Floirac La Souys, three miles east of Bordeaux. Le Castel belongs to a couple named Ledoux, who continue living on the first floor despite the presence of the Rosenbergs. They take over the whole house again after the war and sell the property to the town council during the 1960s.

—

I'd never been to Floirac before and wanted to visit the house that I'd seen only in photographs. It was, after all, where my family spent the beginning of the war.

The Garonne River is gray and overcast that morning in September 2010. After arriving at Bordeaux Mérignac Airport, I cross the river toward Floirac and begin to search for the route de la Tresne, as it is spelled on the family's ration cards. I imagine that the street has been renamed several times by now and soon discover that ever since the socialist council was elected, it's been called avenue du Président François-Mitterrand. Of course . . .

Eventually I find Le Castel, which, according to post-war trial records, was looted during the months following the armistice, under the indulgent eyes of the Ledoux family.

In the middle of a freshly mown lawn stands a cedar, plainly several hundred years old. At the foot of that tree, in May 1940, Henri Matisse and my grandfather engaged in spirited conversations about nature and its representation in painting. Massive, harmonious, reassuring, the tree was perhaps more damaged by the hurricane of 1999 than by the German invasion. The grounds are well tended, while the house itself looks rather weary. It's a curious building, at once charming and distasteful. Designed in the nineteenth century and modeled on a fortress, it combines all the attributes—a keep, stone walls, carved rose windows in the façade—needed to turn it into a sort of Wuthering Heights.

I push open the heavy glass-and-wrought-iron door. The hall looks a bit dingy and clearly hasn't undergone any refurbishment in many years. The big mirror hanging on the wall lends it a certain elegance though the worm-eaten staircase is crumbling into dust.

I climb the shaky stairs and ring the second-floor bell. The door is opened by a startled elderly gentleman, a clerk from the town hall, lodged there by the council. He ushers me into a three- or four-room flat that may have been the bedrooms, and perhaps the dining room, of Le Castel. There's still a dumbwaiter set into one of the walls.

The gentleman listens, slightly baffled, to my babbling ("my family lived here, left in June 1940; I'd like to see the downstairs") and calls the town hall. Two deputies kindly join us and open up the property.

Part of the house hasn't been touched since those days; the other was clearly added on by the Ledoux family over the course of the subsequent decades. Might this work have been paid for, gossips suggested after the war, by the booty hidden inside the house?

Despite its fancy name, the house isn't very big, although the grounds are imposing. I inspect the whole building room by room, saving the drawing room for last. The kitchens are on the ground floor, as they are in all the houses in Haut-Floirac, which were the properties of the affluent Bordeaux bourgeoisie since the end of the nineteenth century. "It dates from the nineteen-thirties or forties," I am told. "The pipes are rusty, the wiring was installed by the occupying Germans," and the office is used as a storeroom for the drinks and mineral water that would be served at private or municipal events.

The Rosenbergs stayed at Le Castel until June 1940, when they decided to flee France. With a clear-eyed view of the deteriorating situation, but perhaps placing too much confidence in the Maginot Line of fortifications against Germany, Paul brought dozens of his paintings to Le Castel so as not to be separated from them, and especially to keep them safe, far from Paris. He rented a vault for them in the town of Libourne, at the Banque Nationale pour le Commerce et l'Industrie (BNCI), which later became the Banque Nationale de Paris, when it was nationalized after the war.

There 162 paintings were stored; they included a van Gogh self-portrait and paintings by Cézanne, Delacroix, Léger, Matisse, Sisley, Picasso, Vuillard, Utrillo, Corot, Monet, and Braque. On September 5, 1941, when the Nazis opened vault number 7, every piece was taken away to the Galerie Nationale du Jeu de Paume. All Göring had to do was seize them.

—

So the Rosenbergs spent the winter of 1940 in Floirac. It was as if time itself had been suspended.

During this period Braque came to visit. Troubled and dispirited about the outbreak of hostilities, he found it difficult to stand before his easel. In October 1939 he wrote to Paul: "I'd started a few canvases, but the turbulence that arose put a stop to all that. I haven't gone back to painting, and for about a month now I've been making sculptures, which I am greatly enjoying. It's athletic work because I've got to bring stones up from the beach that sometimes weigh more than 20 kilos."[1] Clearly, this work was as therapeutic as the defeat was traumatic: 120,000 dead, 200,000 wounded in a few weeks, a people humiliated. "Hitler did in seven weeks what the Germans had dreamed of doing for seventy years."[2]

When the Reich troops arrived in Dieppe, six miles from his property at Varengeville, Braque took his finest paintings and sought temporary refuge with the Rosenbergs in Floriac. He and his wife, Marcelle, also brought with them the little gold in their possession. On Paul's advice, Braque put everything in the vault next to Paul's in the same bank in Libourne. Of course, the vault was later forced open, its contents, along with Paul's paintings, plundered by the Germans.

In 1942 Braque received an almost comical letter from the BNCI about the lock that had been broken by the Nazis and had to be replaced at the bank's expense: "We would be obliged if you would repay the expenses thus accrued—namely, 1,000 francs for expert advice and 200 francs for our trouble."[3]

—

As for Matisse, he moved to Nice.

On July 16, 1939, Matisse and Paul renewed the contract that had bound them together since 1936, adding a clause to the effect that it would become invalid in the event of war. On October 10 Matisse proposed a third contract, a "war contract" to be signed on the thirtieth of the month. "Given the uncertainty of the market, a one-year contract strikes me as reasonable . . . I foresaw a return of the golden age of the arts, a time when artists wouldn't have to put their joys and torments on display . . . delivering their works not as soon as they hatched, but after living with them long enough to see them mature . . . Impossible in the present state of our civilization, and we must resign ourselves to parting company from our children before we've seen them grow," Matisse says, referring to his paintings. "And your indomitable work arrives to rouse me from this state, which is so conducive to meditation even though it is imposed by circumstances. I succumb to temptation; the golden calm remains!"[4]

On both sides, the renewal of this exclusive contract revealed a certain optimism despite everything in the years to come. Paul then announced to Matisse that he wanted to move from Tours to Bordeaux so that his son, Alexandre, "wouldn't yield to idleness" and could continue his studies (Tours was not a university town at the time) and begin his military training.

According to Paul's correspondence, it seems that in Floirac during those first months of 1940, before the catastrophe took place, the passion for art took precedence over commentary on events whose outcome remained uncertain. Many people were apparently unaware of how serious things were. In April 1940 the Art Institute of Chicago had planned a tour for Paul in America, so that he could come, along with his paintings, and deliver lectures on French painting of the nineteenth and twentieth centuries.

That same year, during the so-called Phoney War,* Paul traveled all the way to Nice to see Matisse in his studio and came back by train with canvases under his arm. Clearly enchanted by his visit, he wrote to the painter as soon as he got home. Apparently, hanging his friend's canvases to their greatest advantage was a more pressing

---

*The period from September 3, 1939, to May 10, 1940, after Britain and France had declared war on Germany but before any Western power had mobilized land forces against the German Reich.

matter than seeing his family after his absence: "I found you in a most excellent state . . . I've seen your new works which, the more I think about it, are the very best quality and the very best of Matisse . . . The ones I have brought here were hung on the walls of the living room in Le Castel at 2:30. After contemplating them again, I went to say hello to my family. I was very tired after an 18-hour journey, the sight of your canvases revived me . . . I'm very flattered and honored to have your esteem and trust . . . I'm going to Paris next week, and I will reopen the gallery with five new paintings by Matisse, five by Braque, five by Picasso: what a fine reopening that will be!"[5] But he didn't go back to Paris. The letter is dated April 4, 1940. The German assault on the Ardennes was about to begin.

—

In an article published in Sydney in 1941, the great art critic André Breton was asked to talk about the writers who remained in France during the war, and the magazine, *Art in Australia*, commissioned Paul to try to imagine the lives of his favorite artists under the occupation. Paul described one of his meetings with Matisse, who had, in his turn, come to Floirac just before the German attack.

Their conversation, just a few weeks before the rout, seemed surreal. As usual, they talked about art and painting and contemplated the budding trees and the first flowers to bloom in that spring of 1940. Matisse marveled, Paul relates, at the white and yellow daisies that made the lawn a carpet lovelier than a fourteenth-century tapestry. "That is what we should create," the great colorist told him. "There is the expression of freshness and color that I seek in my canvases. These are the harmonies that nature suggests to us but does not oblige us to reproduce objectively."[6] This was in May 1940.

—

Picasso was in Royan, not far from Floirac.

He and my grandfather went on writing, phoning, seeing each other. Meanwhile, the rest of the family arrived from Paris and crammed themselves into the house. Paul told the Matisses that he would put them up, but there wasn't so much as a free sofa. On June 11, 12, and 13, there were heated family discussions taking place in the ground-floor living room. The Germans had entered Paris on June 10, and the question the family struggled with was whether or not to flee.

Seventy years later, this September afternoon in 2010, here I am back in the same room, with the same fireplace, the same cupboards, and the same chandelier. It's strange watching a scene played out by ghosts. I imagine the evening: chairs crammed together, the children on the parquet floor, the half-packed suitcases in a corner. The room is alive. I hear the sighs, the murmurs, the anxieties, the certainties, the fears of all the people who are there camping out at Le Castel in those days in June 1940.

—

For most French families, there was no question of leaving France, but for some, especially the Jewish ones who knew that they were targets of the Germans and that they were close to the border, the debate was: exile or maintain the status quo.

"Fearful of Vichy, or concerned that they would quickly become pariahs, some French citizens, and also some expatriates living in France, opted to flee," writes Emmanuelle Loyer in *Paris à New York*. "Even the most unwilling began to imagine the possibility of going elsewhere as the noose began to tighten. While the first anti-Jewish statute dates from October 1940, the machinery of exclusion had been set in motion as early as July of that year. Time was short. As David Rousset would later say with gallows humor, France and the rest of Europe would soon offer only two exit routes: Marseille and Auschwitz."[7] Bordeaux might be added to the list.

Jacques Helft, Paul's brother-in-law, was adamant that the family leave France for Portugal, via Spain. As for my grandmother, she was unsure. Paul himself was of two minds. Everyone seemed to be guided by his own temperament when it came to the question of exile. Loyer sums up the dilemma of families by noting the "ultrasensitive balance between the agony of departure and the potentially dramatic implications of the stubborn will to stay." She quotes a letter from Marc Bloch* written in May 1941, stressing the heartache of the historian crushed between "bureaucratic obstructions of the U.S. State Department, family matters and perhaps the growing convictions of the

---

*Historian, founder with Lucien Febvre of the Annales School, and author of one of the finest books about the end of the Third Republic, *L'Étrange défaite*.

author of *L'Étrange défaite* that by remaining in his country one could better serve it."[8] Bloch was shot by the Germans in 1944 near Lyon, where he was in the Resistance.

The problem of passports was the first one that needed to be solved. Seventeen were needed for the Rosenberg family and their dependents, if parents, grandparents, children, brothers, sisters, and nephews were going to get out of France. Marianne, my grandmother Margot's youngest sister, had a childhood friend whose husband, having retreated to Bordeaux with the French government, happened to be secretary to the country's president, Albert Lebrun. Although the republic was stripped of its powers and its territory, it retained the capacity to stamp and validate passports. And this was accomplished. As for the Portuguese consul, he bravely delivered visas, against the will of Portuguese Prime Minister Antonio de Oliveira Salazar.

The second challenge was the crossing of Spain. Franco granted the refugees amassing at the border the right to pass through his country, but not to stop in Spanish territory. Paul and his brothers-in-law ultimately negotiated permission to cross Spain in three days and three nights.

On June 16 they were ready to leave and crammed into the family cars for the trip of approximately 125 miles. Two miles before the border at Hendaye, the controls were strict, and the queue was interminable. They ate butter biscuits, opened sardine tins, and slept in their cars.

Irún, Burgos, Salamanca: as predicted, it took them three days and nights to cross Spain. At the French border, there was a poignant separation from my mother's brother, Alexandre, and his cousins François and Jean, who had decided to stay and fight for their country. They boarded the last Polish ship to leave Bordeaux, the *Batory*—named for a sixteenth-century Polish king—and left Libourne on June 17, 1940. Alexandre was nineteen and had been brought up in the comfort of an affluent family. Why would a young man just past adolescence embark on such an odyssey? The love of his country, a taste for adventure, the need to stand on his own two feet? Exactly what drove my own father to reject a comfortable life in America to go fight in the Middle East?

So Alexandre and his cousins set off even before General de Gaulle issued his landmark appeal for support of the Resistance. As soon as they arrived in Great Britain, they joined what in 1943 would become the Second Armored Division, the Division Blindée of the future hero of the Free French forces, Marshal Philippe Leclerc. On August 24, 1944, my uncle and cousins were among the troops who liberated Paris.

Meanwhile, the rest of the family had reached Portugal and temporarily settled in Sintra, fifteen miles from Lisbon. On a daily basis, the adults laid siege to the consulates and embassies to obtain—the number of refugees in the family had grown by now—twenty-one visas for anywhere: Paraguay, Argentina, Chile. But those visas were extremely precious.[9]* Paul later told an American newspaper

---

*At first, Roosevelt's isolationist America wanted to maintain good relations with the Vichy government and was therefore reluctant to welcome refugees with open arms.

that having arrived in Portugal as a refugee, he went to the British Relief Fund, which gave him a boiled egg and a piece of bread: "Imagine a man who has everything in life . . . and who, a week later, has lost his business, his fortune, his friends. I was sitting on a stone wall with a boiled egg and a crust of bread and I couldn't help laughing."[10]

To be able to board a ship, you needed, as Emmanuelle Loyer writes, to have enough to pay for "a crossing, have a certain reputation, enterprising American friends, or colleagues, a lot of energy and a bit of luck."[11] Not to mention the fact that the Americans' asking refugees to bring some kind of written guarantee that they would be able to earn a living in the United States made it impossible for many to leave.

In August the situation was eased thanks to Paul's old friend Alfred Barr. The distinguished director of the Museum of Modern Art had to fight to explain to the American authorities, who had never or barely heard of Paul Rosenberg, the potential artistic advantage that the United States might gain by welcoming him onto its soil. Barr was a persuasive man, and the Rosenbergs managed to obtain those precious visas. The Helft family (my grandparents' sisters, brothers-in-law, and cousins) received theirs four days later.

Thanks to various networks, between three and four thousand French citizens managed to reach the United States in this way. On September 20, 1940, Paul and his family disembarked in New York. They were lucky: about 75,000 French citizens died in Nazi concentration camps.

Seventy years later my visit to Floirac brings their exodus chillingly to life. I now understand why my mother never wanted to see that house again, even though it would be her last link with France for five years.

I too am more unsettled by the house than I'd anticipated. I must be visibly shaken, because the mayor's deputies suggest stopping off at the town hall, just around the corner, for a glass of water. It's oppressively hot. The mayor, Conchita Lacuey, who is also the Socialist Party deputy of the Gironde, the department that includes Bordeaux, drops in to greet me warmly, to tell me how amazed she is by life's coincidences, and turns the moment into a photo opportunity. "You never know," she says, on that late-summer day. Her own grandparents, hard-line republicans, arrived from Spain more or less as my fleeing family was entering the country.

AT THE
CENTRE POMPIDOU

The war and the mark that it left on our house on rue La Boétie, the conditions under which my family stayed in Floirac, and finally their desperate quest for refuge in the United States are consuming me.

I need to retrace my steps, to get back to the very core of things, to my grandfather's work, and to scour the family archives. I plan to immerse myself in them when I am in New York, though I am mostly living in Washington, D.C., at this point. But on a visit to Paris, I take the opportunity to call the Centre Georges Pompidou, to see if its archives have any information about my grandfather.

After a chilly reception from the director, Alfred Pacquement, I am welcomed more warmly by Didier Schulmann, who is in charge of the Kandinsky Library. We arrange a meeting for May 10. May 10? The twenty-ninth anniversary of Mitterrand's victory? What's the connection? Only that which leads from politics to modern art and back again.

Unfortunately, there's nothing much of interest about my grandfather in the museum, Schulmann tells me, except for some photographic plates that are stored off-site. I have another pleasant interview with one of the curators at the Centre Pompidou, Christian Derouet, who was responsible for the Kandinsky exhibition there several years ago. Derouet worked for a long time on Léonce Rosenberg's archives and told me he'd come across Léonce's brother, Paul, in the course of his research.

The reception I get from M. Pacquement indicates that he still bears a certain degree of rancor toward my family, which had some ten years before retrieved from the Centre Pompidou basement a painting stamped "MNR, Musées Nationaux Récupération: National Museums Recovery."* At the time the museum had been unwilling to return that painting by Fernand Léger, *Woman in Red and Green*, also called *Knight in Armor*, on the pretext that the museum directors didn't know whether the painting, which they acknowledged had been stolen from rue La Boétie, belonged to Paul or to Léonce. So the court decided, quite logically, that if there was any doubt, the painting should go to both families and that the heirs—my mother, my aunt, and Léonce's descendants—were to share the work, as was done without difficulty. It was understandable enough that the Centre Pompidou didn't know to which part of the family it should restore

---

*A formula applied to works of art recovered from the Nazis and kept in the national museums while their owners were not yet identified.

the painting, and it wasn't hard to grasp its unwillingness to part with such a beautiful work of art.

Because it was not realistic for all the Rosenberg cousins to share the painting, a decision was made to sell it. I wasn't very interested in it at the time since I'd barely been aware of the research done by my family, especially my aunt and cousins in New York, who had sought the painting's retrieval. But I do remember my mother's telling me about the strange feeling she had had as she gazed at that painting, which was completely new to her, its having passed through the gallery without her ever setting eyes on it.

I subsequently learned that between September 1939 and June 1940 my mother and her parents had left Paris, but Léonce, my grandfather's brother, hadn't wanted to follow them. He spent the war in the capital, proudly wearing his yellow star, and miraculously escaped the roundup before dying in 1947. A great discoverer of new talent but always penniless, he often asked my grandfather for money in return for paintings that he owned and stored at rue La Boétie. That was what happened during the winter of 1939–40, in a transaction with Paul, who was based in Floirac. Léonce received a wire transfer from his brother and put his Léger in Paul's gallery, where it was stolen in July 1940, when the property was handed over to the Germans and a few French opportunists. Subsumed by the state after the war, *Woman in Red and Green* slumbered peacefully at the Centre Pompidou, labeled "MNR," while neither the family nor the museum were aware of its resting place.

—

Though there are no archives on my grandfather at the Centre Pompidou, I am granted exceptional permission to consult the photographic plates taken in the family gallery, which are kept in the Kandinsky Library archives in one of the museum's warehouses. All collections not on display have been transferred to massive storerooms for fear that a flood, which seems to happen every hundred years or so, might once again inundate the basements of the Paris museums, as happened in 1910.

It's the largest of those great warehouses, or at least the one that houses the treasures of the Musée d'Art Moderne that aren't on display. Mile after mile, seemingly endless avenues are filled with mysteriously numbered crates containing sculptures that may never have been seen by anyone. Great cabinets mounted on wheels contain countless paintings that remain hidden from the human eye. Dozens of unmounted canvases on rollers, like the shelves in a rug showroom. I spot a Warhol and a Miró crying out to be hung.

In another high-security section behind a reinforced double door, for which you need a special badge to enter, I step inside the rooms where the photographic archives are kept. There are thousands of glass plates, all meticulously cataloged. A number of filing boxes represent the Paul Rosenberg collection. My mother and my uncle donated it to the Ministry of Culture in 1973 to grant researchers access to the works in their original state. Here they are, dusty and fragile, like memory itself. Dozens of cartons marked Bissière,* Braque, Laurencin, Matisse, and Léger hold heavy plates of glass, artifacts of a photographic process used before the war. Most were taken by a famous art photographer at the time who went by the name Routhier and are of peerless quality.

In those prints I see the exhibition halls that I recently visited at rue La Boétie, the paneling reaching halfway up the wall and the unmistakable glass ceiling with its little star-shaped windows. The black-and-white photographs look strange, given that these are such famous and vivid paintings, but the prints are so magical that you can almost imagine they're in full color.

The glass plates that move me most are the ones commemorating exhibitions by Matisse or Braque in the late thirties, probably because I've seen other photographs taken only a few months later in the same settings; only this time the paintings of the two great masters have been replaced by the portrait of Pétain and violently anti-Semitic slogans.

I open these boxes more or less at random and delicately lift the pictures from their yellowed envelopes, those plates of glass so fragile that some of them are broken or cracked. The cracks disturb me: Is it just the damage wrought by time, or is it abuse by the occupying forces that pilfered them? Perhaps it doesn't matter; the

*A French painter contemporary with Braque and Gris, whose first exhibition was held at the Rosenberg Gallery in 1921.

damage cannot be reversed. And deep in the recesses of the archives, the past somehow feels beyond reach. Why only now do I want to know who my grandfather was, what kind of person he was, how he lived? Why only now am I exploring his world?

GENNEVILLIERS

I decide to try to visit all the places where my family's memory is preserved. So: to the furniture depository where I've stored most of the papers and photographs that I hurriedly gathered from my mother's house after her death. It's freezing in this big unit at Gennevilliers, where moving men bring in the containers on casters and open them up in my presence, as in a morgue. Why do I feel like a gravedigger, when emptying my mother's cupboards did not make me feel that way?

I set off again quickly, very quickly, with a big cardboard box in the trunk of my car, chosen from the twenty-five or so boxes that had been stored. I'll spend the next two nights sifting through photographs and letters. Most of these chests contain the papers of France Forever, of which my mother was secretary-general. The U.S.-based information organization was set up to relay to the Americans the efforts of the Free French and the Resistance. In 1940 and 1941, before Franklin Roosevelt entered the war, the Americans needed proof that the French deserved to be helped and weren't just a nation that had simply capitulated to the occupying forces, as it was fashionable to write in the 1960s and 1970s. Emmanuelle Loyer speaks about France Forever as "an association set up on the initiative of a group of French who had settled in the United States, to 'drum up sympathy and material help for Free France.'"[1]

I unwrap these relics as if they were remnants of a vanished world: a Cross of Lorraine (de Gaulle's symbol of resistance); a photograph of General de Gaulle signed to my mother, Micheline Rosenberg, which she kept even after becoming a fervent anti-Gaulliste. And the collection of pamphlets published by France Forever, written and designed by my mother.

I feel guilty. She would have loved me to have shown an interest in her wartime efforts while she was alive. And yet I'd always found her glorification of France Forever a bit tiresome. I'd even told her, dismissively, in that sullen teenage way, that Roosevelt had entered the war only because of Pearl Harbor and that it certainly had nothing to do with France Forever. This wasn't necessarily untrue, but it was cruel to try to disparage her work as an activist and to prefer the heroes of the shadows that clashed in Kiev or skirmished in the desert.

For my mother, the war years in New York were—shocking though it may seem—captivating. Though they were not the happiest years of her life, they were certainly the most fulfilling. These were the years when she had genuinely exciting tasks to perform, ones to which she had committed herself completely, with talent and imagination.

From the boxes I take notebooks and drafts of letters and reports, wondering how such an intelligent woman could allow herself to be locked away in a conventional life of marriage and motherhood without ever searching for the freedom and the friends she missed once the war was over. Such a life seemed such a waste to the young woman that I was in the 1970s and 1980s. For me, as for my contemporaries who tried to "have it all," that conventional way of being was out of the question.

In addition to these notebooks, these brochures emblazoned with red, white, and blue rosettes, Lorraine crosses, and editorials dissecting the ideological differences between General de Gaulle and General Henri Giraud (who was preferred by the Americans since they mistrusted the head of the Free French), I find a treasure trove of personal papers and letters.

I stay up till the small hours sorting and filing that huge archive: heating bills from the Floirac residence at the beginning of the war; ration cards from the Gironde in 1940 and Paris in 1945; the rulings from cases brought—and won—by my family against certain vultures; letters from Léger or Matisse to my grandfather from 1939—so many other letters! My grandfather's tiny, slanting handwriting, expressing a little bit of himself.

These letters date both from the war and from the years that followed and reveal the grand obsession of Paul's life: his paintings, which he loved as if they were living beings. For him, their recovery after the war, a source of so much anguish, reflected his determination to see his rights acknowledged and to ensure that his children would have a comfortable life. There is much humility in these letters, and some shy and tender outpourings to his son, Alexandre, who relieved him of the worry of running the gallery during the 1950s; to his daughter, Micheline, who lived far away in Paris; and to me, his granddaughter, whom he called "my darling sweetie."

—

There are heaps of photographs, all quite unreal to me. In this picture, the thin, distant-looking old man of my childhood appears young and gaunt. He is wearing a sleeveless bathing costume in a swimming pool in Monte Carlo (necessarily elegant). He is teaching my mother to dive. Or in 1930 he is with his wife and two children skating at Saint Moritz (elegant, always elegant), in baggy Tintin-style trousers, his hair blowing in the wind.

Was he tender? Was he cheerful, my grandfather who was a father first and foremost, a papa who asked his children to call him by his first name? That shocked the gentle Marguerite Blanchot, who worked for my grandparents for fifty years and who always said, "People will say that Monsieur is not the children's father!"

In fact, Paul was an anxious and shy man who relaxed more easily in his letters to his beloved daughter than in his conversations with her.

—

During the 1950s, and throughout his life, Paul complained with less and less detachment about his health, which was poor, and about his business, which was actually thriving but which he thought was in a terrible state. He worried about political instability in France and about the Korean War, which he thought might worsen at any moment. He pleaded with my mother to come back to New York with my father and me for our own safety and suggested leaving for Argentina, which was described by relatives who had emigrated there as the new El Dorado. To Argentina, like so many former Nazis? To flee again, when there was no real threat? To resume the immigrant lifestyle, in a remote corner of the world, farther from a danger that had already passed?

Sanity prevailed. Having set off on a reconnaissance trip to Juan Perón's Buenos Aires, Paul came back posthaste and made us unpack all the suitcases that stood in the hallway. Had he sensed that the country, once the richest in South America, was about to go into decline, into a period of galloping inflation under a series of bloody dictatorships?

He remained concerned about the future, finding little relief or reassurance in the fact that the nightmare was now over. It was as if with each successive international event, his identity and his family's might once more be called into question. The letters were largely devoted to the arrangements he wanted to make so that my mother and her brother could keep the gallery running, reflecting his life's work: the need to introduce people to contemporary culture, to make them understand it, to spread its message in a barbaric world.

He asked Alexandre to develop and manage this gallery, and my uncle did so scrupulously until his death in

1987. As for his sister, my mother, she had to defer to Alexandre, to place blind trust in his instincts for running the business. And above all, the two Rosenberg children were supposed to remain united. In fact, my uncle Alexandre fulfilled the promise he made to his father so loyally that he often took greater care of his sister than he did of his own family.

Alexandre was an aesthete, the first president of the Art Dealers Association of America, and a connoisseur in great demand for the infallibility of his eye. His family— his wife, cousins, sister, niece—called him Kiki, the nickname his parents had given him when he was born in 1921 in the apartment at rue La Boétie, with Picasso as witness. They probably wouldn't have guessed that this childish nickname would later be applied to a very serious man behind a pair of tortoiseshell glasses. Although he retained his French nationality, Alexandre eventually married an American woman, my aunt Elaine, and became a true New Yorker. Yet he remained attached to French culture and was keen that his children, my cousins Elisabeth and Marianne, take advantage of their dual nationality to pursue their higher education in Paris.

Unlike his father, Alexandre had embarked on his journey through the art world more out of filial duty than his own personal taste, which inclined more toward literature, philosophy, and fifteenth-century incunabula. He was less sociable than his father—more brusque—and while his love of art was limitless, his love of commerce was not. So much so that after my grandfather's death the Galerie Paul Rosenberg lost its dynamism and relied on its existing inventory. Though the two families were kept very comfortable for more than fifty years, the holdings gradually dwindled. Of the more than three hundred works recovered from the original collection, four major works have stayed with me.

—

I knew my uncle well but still have trouble envisioning Paul, his father, who lived through the final years of the nineteenth century and the first exhilarating yet tragic half of the twentieth. I have to banish the anxiety-ridden letters written at the end of his life and imagine what must have given him joy: to discover works of artistic genius by his contemporaries and to become entwined with their stories. I must immerse myself in his world, the world of a passionate and original art dealer.

DEALER

For a long time the language of the dealer irritated me. Words like "objets d'art," or "rare and beautiful things," to quote the phrase on the façade of the Musée de l'Homme, made me cringe. If my grandfather had sold jeans or tins of sardines, I wouldn't have considered it unseemly, but when I was young, getting rich by trading in objets d'art carried the same sulfurous whiff as the banking profession does today. Nothing dishonest, exactly, but an "impure" quality amplified by the French disdain for money.

The image of bohemian painters dying in garrets made me mistrust the trade of those who prospered from selling paintings. The idea of commerce, of trade, of buying canvases from indigent painters before selling them at a considerable profit troubled me. Julius II ensuring the glory of Michelangelo or Peggy Guggenheim buying a painting a day: these were noble efforts to preserve the arts.

On the other hand, I would have been hugely impressed by a man motivated entirely by the love of art, a kind of patron whose raison d'être was the survival of good taste and the disinterested promotion of penniless young artists.

And then I got older. I learned that the world according to Proudhon exists mostly in books, that making money isn't necessarily a sin (that is, if you don't exploit anybody), that you might even consider it moral to produce wealth rather than simply benefit from the wealth of society.

So yes, my grandfather Paul Rosenberg was a dealer. It wasn't a new profession. Rembrandt bid up the prices of his paintings at public sales in order to increase the value of artists' work. Bernini did the same in the seventeenth century. Vincent van Gogh and Paul Gauguin also understood the workings of the market. Ambroise Vollard wasn't just an intermediary for the impressionists; he wasn't just the dealer of Cézanne and Gauguin: he was also their advocate. Paul Durand-Ruel was another who knew how to create interest in his beloved impressionists, engaging qualities transcending those of the mere businessman.

Paul was a dealer, just as they were, a successful dealer, even though his aesthetic judgments governed his decisions more than a desire for commercial success. Certainly, his passion for modern painting developed gradually. The same was true of Daniel-Henry Kahnweiler, whose biographer Pierre Assouline says that his attachment to contemporary art was not apparent at the start of his career. Kahnweiler was a banker who knew little about art, and his fascination with the painters of his day was "the fruit of a slow process of maturation," an apprenticeship.[1]

The parallel between the two men is interesting, given the importance of their respective images in the art world. Kahnweiler was a gifted art dealer who first set up his business during the early years of the twentieth century, but whose success was finally established after the Second World War, according to Assouline. A character not very dissimilar, in my view, to Paul: "sober," "imperious," "tough in his professional dealings," "a bit old-fashioned," "sensitive to the slightest hint of fawning, and enormously proud."[2]

Their backgrounds were quite similar, one from a family of art dealers only recently arrived in France from Bratislava, the other from a German banking family; both members of a bourgeois class sheltered from material hardship. Both men understood the revolution in twentieth-century painting, although Paul's tastes inclined toward Picasso and Braque, while Kahnweiler was drawn more to Juan Gris, his great friend, and to Maurice de Vlaminck. Both men refused to show the surrealist painters in their galleries, asserting that while surrealism was legitimate and innovative in literary terms, it was not sufficiently pictorial. Both dealers completely ignored Salvador Dalí and Max Ernst, Joan Miró and René Magritte.* Neither man was willing to write a memoir. Paul considered it vulgar and inappropriate to

---

*One day when Salvador Dalí politely approached Paul in a restaurant to ask him to represent him, Paul's reply was harsh, crude, and lacking in vision: "Monsieur, my gallery is a serious institution, not made for clowns."

dwell on himself, while Kahnweiler set out his life story in broad terms in his book on Gris.

There the similarities end. The differences are many.

First of all, their relationship to the wars. Paul had been a soldier, mobilized in 1914, and very concerned about what was going on politically in the 1930s. He campaigned against the acquisition of the art that was being sold off cheaply by the Nazis, and was forced to flee his country in 1940, hunted by the Germans. Kahnweiler, on the other hand, had been an ardent pacifist, refusing—and this took courage—to fight for either side in the First World War. He was thoroughly anti-Nazi, but did not believe in a second world war right up to the eve of Hitler's invasion of Poland, and managed to hide in France between 1940 and 1944. He sold his gallery to his sister-in-law Louise Leiris, a Burgundian Catholic, and was somehow able to maintain his place within the establishment under the occupation.

Paul's and Kahnweiler's careers also took different trajectories: my grandfather, who had made a name for himself in impressionist painting, rose to fame in the world of modern art after the First World War. Kahnweiler was initiated into contemporary art earlier, at the very start of the twentieth century, and carved out a fine reputation for himself fairly quickly. But then he spent a long period in the shadows before returning with full strength in 1945. By that time Paul was far beyond the shores of France.

Paul quickly developed a sense that the United States would overtake Europe both in the art market and in terms of cultural excitement. From 1922 onward he set about awakening Americans to the exhilaration of modern art. Kahnweiler was still convinced that Paris was the global art capital, and he maintained his belief in the supremacy of old Europe until he died in 1979.

The century's turbulence affected the two men in similar ways: the Second World War cut Paul off from his artists, just as the First World War had done for Kahnweiler. Much the same may be said of their success: Paul's fame in the art world exploded only after the First World War was over. Kahnweiler's triumph came chiefly after the liberation, when he won back his representation of the painters who had left him during the 1920s, becoming, most important of all, Picasso's exclusive dealer.

On a personal level, the two men did not get on well. There are no records of any unpleasant remarks from Paul about Kahnweiler, but Pierre Assouline portrays the subject of his biography as harsh in his treatment of all his colleagues, notably my grandfather. He was probably angry and hurt about the behavior of Paul's brother Léonce, who had attracted the cubist painters to his gallery while Kahnweiler was exiled in Switzerland during the First World War. Besides, Léonce's reputation was tarnished by the fact that he had agreed, during the 1920s, to be an expert consultant in the liquidation of Kahnweiler's property, which had been confiscated by the French because of his German citizenship. But the severity of Assouline's subject also seems to extend to Paul, whom Kahnweiler treated with a degree of contempt.

Paul, who had chosen to sell nineteenth-century canvases so that he could buy twentieth-century works and thereby provide his artists with a livelihood, decided to put more money than his colleagues did into funding the painters he represented. He wanted to pay his artists (notably Picasso, Braque, Léger, and Matisse) handsomely, in order to give them the freedom to paint. Kahnweiler, whom Picasso may have aptly described as miserly, made it a point of honor not to pay his artists more than he had to and never to bid up prices.

When Léger came to him and said, "Paul Rosenberg gives me twice what you do," Kahnweiler replied, "Very well, then, go to Rosenberg."[3] So in the 1920s and 1930s, after Picasso, Braque, Léger, and even, for a time in 1930, André Masson, signed with Paul, de Vlaminck left for Bernheim-Jeune, and André Derain for Paul Guillaume. Kahnweiler was left only with his beloved Juan Gris, in perpetual rivalry with Picasso and other less important painters.

It is easy to imagine why Kahnweiler might have been bitter, but Paul had opted to pursue a policy that favored contemporary artists, providing them with both fame and material comfort. And he was one of those who embodied the golden age of French painting between the wars. This is the central thesis put forward by Michael C. FitzGerald, who writes that "the market was not peripheral to the development of modernism but central to it."[4]

If Picasso's painting took off in the 1920s, it did so not least because Paul knew how to promote the painter and guide him in directions other than cubism. Paul also understood that it was important to view Picasso's work in the context of the tumultuous forces of the twentieth century and French painting of the past. This was more important, in the end, than constantly promoting cubism. As the American press has often pointed out, Paul was, until the war, the biggest art dealer in Europe, dealing in a wide range of artists, from Delacroix to Picasso. "Imagine," a major California newspaper wrote in the 1940s, "being able to step inside Matisse or Picasso's studio twice a year, being allowed to look at forty of their best paintings and saying, 'I'll take the lot!' Until the War broke out, that was just what Paul Rosenberg did."[5]

Finally, Kahnweiler and Rosenberg differed in their attitude toward museums. Kahnweiler was surely resentful about the confiscation of his property and, believing that he had already been forced to give quite enough to the state against his will, "didn't like to give to museums. It was beyond the limit of his generosity."[6] Paul, on the other hand, was overly generous. Grateful to America for welcoming him as a refugee in 1940, he gave large numbers of paintings (by artists including Picasso, Renoir, and van Gogh) to American museums in New York and elsewhere. After the war, happy to have recovered many of his stolen paintings, he gave the French state, including the Musée d'Art Moderne in Paris, roughly thirty large and beautiful works.

—

At the start of the 1950s, Paul's innovative tendencies were still in evidence when he signed a contract with Nicolas de Staël, for example, or in his attempt to launch the paintings of Le Corbusier, which never really caught on. He also made forays into American painting previously known only to a select circle, such as the works of Max Weber, Karl Knaths, and Abraham Rattner.

But he never moved on to the next stage, which might have led him, during his lifetime, to two very different types of contemporary painter, Edward Hopper and Willem de Kooning. He probably wouldn't have liked Jasper Johns or Mark Rothko, had he come across them. And he would not have inclined toward the pop art of Robert Rauschenberg or Andy Warhol. Everyone has his or her own limits in the appreciation of modernity.

For its December 1941–January 1942 issue, *Art in Australia* had, as we have seen, asked Paul to articulate his vision of painting and speak about the painters who had stayed behind in France during the war. Having arrived in the United States only a year before, Paul was presented as the man best acquainted with the artists of the previous era. "Painters before their time do not exist," he said. "They are always of their epoch. It is the public who is ever behind in the pictorial revolution. The public eagerly accepts the formula of a 'recent past' when it has been definitively accepted, but refuses to regard or even attempt to understand that of their immediate present. How many errors have been committed, and how many great young painters have been forced to know misery because of the buyer's ignorance and his refusal to support them; refusal because they 'don't like that aspect' or because they 'do not understand' . . . Too often the spectator looks for arguments within himself against the works rather than attempting to free himself from those conventions which he believes he understands, agrees with and likes."[7]

—

In a similar spirit, there was an article that Paul always kept close at hand, so that he could refer to it often, notably using it as an appendix to the catalog of the last big exhibition that he devoted to Picasso in Paris in 1936. It's a delightful piece by Albert Wolff, an art critic from the early years of the Third Republic, which was published in *Le Figaro* in 1876. The "impressionists," a term that was intended as an insult, but that the artists themselves brandished as a badge of honor, had made headlines just two years before, and curators had trouble accepting the genius of something they couldn't understand. Paul kept this text as an antidote to the incomprehension of his contemporaries:

"Rue Le Peletier is suffering great misfortune. After the fire at the Opéra, here comes another disaster crashing down on the neighborhood. An exhibition, said to be of paintings, has just opened at Durand-Ruel . . . There are people who explode with laughter when they see such things. As for me, it makes me heartsick. These so-called artists call themselves the intransigents, the impressionists; they take canvases, paint and brushes, throw on a few colors and sign the thing. So it is that at the Ville-Evrard, lost souls are gathering pebbles along their way and imagining they have found diamonds . . . So please be so kind as to inform M. Pissaro [*sic*] that the trees are not purple, that the sky is not the color of fresh butter, that in no country will you see the things he paints . . . Try to make M. Degas see reason . . . Try to explain to M. Renoir that a woman's torso is not a heap of decomposing flesh with purple and green patches denoting the state of complete putrefaction of a corpse! . . . And it's this pile of vulgarities that is being displayed in public with no thought for the fatal consequences that they might provoke! Yesterday, on rue Le Peletier, they arrested a poor man who, leaving this exhibition, was biting passersby."[8] The article is well enough written, the charge is effectively leveled, but the mockery was turned against its author a few decades later.

—

Paul was combatting precisely this sort of thinking. But was he a visionary or merely—and this in itself would be something—going along with innovative painters and showing their work alongside the masters of the previous century in order to gain acceptance for the modernists? How daring was he, really? How did he see the role of an art dealer in a profession that was rapidly becoming organized?

After the war he wrote to Lucienne, Léonce's daughter, who wanted to open a gallery herself: "Don't make the same mistake as your poor father did, restricting yourself to very avant-garde painting. Mix up your exhibitions in such a way that they attract the whole of your clientele, the part of it that considers itself advanced and the other, more conservative part. Maintaining without money a policy entirely ahead of its time is a cul-de-sac. These things have to be done gradually."[9]

—

That was basically how Paul started out, like his own father before him.

My great-grandfather Alexandre was a grain merchant. A long way from the world of art. When he was nearly ruined by a cargo of rotten goods, he decided to put his last savings into the thing that he really loved, "objets d'art and curiosities." Farewell to the grain trade. He became an antiques dealer, at 38 avenue de l'Opéra.

I remember looking at the building's façade indifferently. It's at the end of the avenue, practically on the place de l'Opéra, one of those buildings that now house insurance companies and airlines. I still have trouble imagining an art gallery in this setting, a place that seems designated for trade, for the tourists, in the shadow of the Palais Garnier.

One day, turning up early at the Salle Drouot, my great-grandfather, who had recently become an art dealer, bought a painting he liked for 87.50 francs. It was a Sisley, the first impressionist painting he brought home, and at a time when practically everyone, apart from Vollard and more particularly Durand-Ruel, was ignoring this new artistic school. The great battles fought to win it recognition were drawing to a close, but still the public hadn't come. Intrigued, my great-grandfather went on to discover Manet, Monet, and Renoir.

It was probably this that reconciled me to the word "dealer." Coming from nowhere, my great-grandfather trained his eye, trusting his own instincts, his own daring taste. So was it really about commerce, if the canvases that he bought—and that sold badly—were the work of illustrious unknowns? It seemed a passion first and foremost, a calling that had become a profession.

—

"One day when I was about ten, my father led me to the shop window of a dealer who kept a gallery on the rue Le Peletier, to show me a painting that made me shriek with horror," writes my grandfather in the fragment of an autobiography that he began during the war years in New York. "Imagine a very thickly painted picture made with violent colors, representing a modest bedroom with a wooden bed covered with a red blanket, an ordinary wooden table with a water jug, a bowl and, hanging from the walls, shapeless old clothes. The floor looked oddly bowed to me, and the furniture seemed to be dancing, as if it wanted, as in a cartoon, to leap off the canvas and fly out through the window. My father calmed me down and said, 'I don't know this artist, and the canvas isn't signed, but I'm going to find out about him because I'd like to buy some of his paintings.' The canvas [*Room in Arles*] was by van Gogh, it's the one that's in the Art Institute of Chicago, and which, by an irony of fate, I myself sold about 30 years later."

The impressionists, van Gogh, Cézanne: this was where all of my great-grandfather's savings ended up, much to the distress of his wife. "My mother"—Paul continues in his sketch of a family memoir—"claimed her husband had gone mad and that he was ruining his children. 'What are our friends and customers going to think?' she groaned. Her dismay reached its peak when a van Gogh and a Cézanne came into the house. She would call upstairs, 'Children, your father's going completely mad: he's buying *vann Govoghs* and *Ces Anes*.' It's true that everyone who came to the house, even collectors and connoisseurs, guffawed at the sight of a blue or yellow Monet, saying that no one knew an equivalent in nature. One day, we were having lunch when the phone rang. My father picked it up. 'How much do I want for my Cézanne? 6,000 francs, I can't go any lower than that. So you'll take it?' He was delighted to be able to show his wife that there was someone even crazier than he was!"

So the impressionists entered the home of Rosenberg *père*, at a time when not many art lovers were interested in them, and when dealers themselves preferred to sell paintings by the Barbizon school. Works by Monet, Manet, Pissarro, Sisley, Courbet, Daumier, Toulouse-Lautrec, Cézanne, and van Gogh now decorated the gallery on the avenue de l'Opéra. Renoir too, whose *A Girl with a Watering Can* my great-grandfather acquired, a painting that my grandfather sold much later to the great American collector Chester Dale. It was the first painting, and one of the most beautiful, in the series hung in the National

Gallery of Art in Washington, D.C., at the impressive exhibition of the Chester Dale collection in 2009.

I went there to see if it was as graceful as its familiar reproduction and was dazzled by the sun that illuminates the child's blond hair, bringing alive the shadows on her cheeks.

CHÂTEAUDUN, OPÉRA, AND MADISON AVENUE

I have found Paul's torn and yellowed birth certificate: he was born on December 29, 1881, in the Ninth Arrondissement of Paris, in rue de Châteaudun, the son of Alexandre Rosenberg and Mathilde Jellinck. The strange-sounding names come from Hungary—Bratislava, in fact, which is now the capital of Slovakia and was at the time part of the Austro-Hungarian Empire.

My mother always said proudly—no doubt a legacy of the traumas of 1940—that she had been French for two generations. And yet that's somewhat inaccurate: her father, even though he was actually born in France, wasn't automatically French by birth. The law of June 26, 1889, which sought to grant full citizenship to all children born on French soil, applied to children born in France of foreign parents, but only once they had reached their maturity. So in 1902, when he turned twenty-one, Paul should have applied for naturalization. But at the time he was in London learning his trade, and he let the deadline slip. Is it possible that our family's national identity has been imperiled since the start of the twentieth century?

So it is that I find, in my dusty boxes, a second piece of paper from 1913, reminding Paul that he had to apply for naturalization if he wanted to become a French citizen. The paper is signed by Louis Barthou, who was the minister of justice at the time and was killed in Marseille in 1934 by a stray bullet during the attempted assassination of Alexander of Yugoslavia by the Ustashe.

Although he was born in Paris, my grandfather became French as the result of will in a France that, on the brink of the First World War, was keen to call up as many of its young men as possible. In short, my Frenchness is fairly recent on that side of the family. There were, at this time of the Third Republic, no French laws especially favorable to the children of immigrants.

—

Paul joins his father's business in January 1898, at the age of sixteen. "He wanted me to learn the trade while I was still young. He started by making me copy out letters and file them. After eight days, I told him I'd only keep on doing that when I'd finished my art studies. He agreed, and here I am running around museums, taking notes."[1] He begins by studying the arts of antiquity—of the Chaldeans, Egyptians, Greeks—before ending up with the moderns. During the holidays he travels around the museums of Europe and ends up well acquainted with them. "Knowing the primitives, having studied their expression, their writings, the modes of expression they had adopted, allowed me to understand at a very young age that there was no process, that all that mattered was the laws of construction, relationships of values, volumes, lines and what it was that they wanted to express . . . I went out with my father, who initiated me into the antique dealer's trade and corrected my impressions. I became presumptuous and criticized the artistic purchases he made without me."

For better or worse, however, he is learning. "We had an old china dinner set, pink background, and we had a barrel in the same color. One day one of our clients, the Prince de St. L., came to the house and I sold him the set, including the barrel, which cost on its own more than the rest of the set. Amazed by the price, the buyer insisted on taking the pieces away in person. Very proud of the sale, I told my father, who called me all the names of the day and declared that I would never be fit for the trade! I must admit that I wasn't proud of my beginnings as a businessman."

But over time his eye improves, and Paul thinks he's made it. "Because you know your way around," his father tells him, "go to London, open a gallery, do some business and try not to make any mistakes." So the young man sets off at the age of nineteen, sure that he will be lavishly praised upon his return. "Alas, my first experiences were no more successful. Without my father, I had no one to guide me." Looking for paintings by the rather academic Belgian painter Alfred Stevens, he hurries to buy a work by an A. Stevens, who turns out to be Agrippa rather than Alfred, that has no commercial value whatsoever. But he soon makes progress. He buys two Monets for 250 pounds, two drawings by van Gogh for 40, and wins the trust of his father. Having retired from dealing in objets d'art to devote himself entirely to paintings, Alexandre hopes that his sons will become dealers in paintings in turn.

In 1906 Alexandre, now in poor health, sets up his two sons at 38 avenue de l'Opéra, where Paul realizes that selling the impressionists isn't going to bring in enough to earn a living. "We were forced to buy 'salable' paintings." By this he means the Barbizon School, which continues to dominate the taste of the times. Still, Paul tries unsuccessfully to sell a painting by the Barbizon painter Félix Ziem to a buyer who thinks that six thousand francs for a view of Venice with a crooked campanile is pretty steep. He also tries to off-load a portrait of Louis XIV on a descendant of the Bourbons, who is disappointed when Paul naively tells him that he doesn't look a bit like his ancestor.

"I was successful, but I was troubled by the idea that I was selling paintings I didn't like, certain that they wouldn't be recognized in the future. It was then that I determined to sell everything I owned and invest in the impressionists. I realized that if I were going to compete with the big auction houses of the day, I needed to buy only the highest-quality works, and rely on time to make a name for myself."

These were in fact the two lessons that he drew from his apprenticeship and put to good use some years later. First repeating, with modifications, his experience with the impressionists, he deliberately chose to sell paintings that he truly loved and waited for art lovers to recognize their beauty. Over the course of ten years and two distinct phases, he moved from the Barbizon School to the works of Pablo Picasso. He would bide his time.

From that moment on, he forged the reputation that stayed with him throughout his life. In forty years, from Paris to New York, from his father's gallery on avenue de l'Opéra, to his own near Madison Avenue, his imprimatur was the absolute quality of the works he sold.

But his passion for the modernists never allowed him to forget his great love of Renoir. Sometime ago, in Paris, I forced myself to go to the Grand Palais to see the exhibition of late Renoirs, the ones he painted at the start of the last century. I confess to finding Renoir's paintings facile, more tiresome than enchanting, perhaps because they have been reproduced once too often, printed on a thousand-and-one posters, tea towels, or place mats. It's a bit like a lover of classical music's not wanting to hear Mozart's Forty-first Symphony—the *Jupiter*—for the umpteenth time, after it's been played over and over again by every orchestra on the planet.

I was convinced that Renoir's late style—vague, reddish, and allegorical—debased the oeuvre of his glorious years. A judgment inherited, I believed, from Paul and then passed on to me by my mother, it struck me as irrefutable.

And yet that exhibition, *Renoir in the Twentieth Century*, was a real gift. It brought together the paintings from 1880 to 1890, when Renoir was distancing himself from the impressionist revolution, painting *en plein air*, in favor of a series of portraits of sweet, dreamy girls: Gabrielle—his son Jean's nanny—with her charming profile; bathers at their toilet; scenes of ordinary bourgeois life (girls doing their hair, reading, sewing, or taking piano lessons); voluptuous nudes not unlike those of Boucher or Rubens. Among the very last paintings was *Les Baigneuses*, given to the state by Renoir's sons in 1923, just after his death. I don't like this painting, although Renoir himself called it a "success" and a "springboard for experiments to come." I don't like his soft, fleshy odalisques and as a result agreed with the blunt judgment of Renoir's work that my family history attributed to Paul.

I say "attributed" because the exhibition finished with a big surprise: a whole wall covered with huge photographs of the 1934 exhibition that Paul had devoted to Renoir in his gallery, showing a selection of the canvases from the painter's last years. In it I saw all the paintings that were the real treasures of the retrospective at the Grand Palais, including those *baigneuses* that seem so flabby and pink to me today.

And it was one of those canvases, known by its American name, *Reclining Nude*, that my grandparents donated to the Museum of Modern Art in New York in 1956, the first painting by Renoir to enter that museum, which sold it only a few years ago to buy a van Gogh, since American museums have the right to buy and sell the works in their collection. And it was one of the stellar paintings at the big Renoir exhibition at the Grand Palais in September 2009, one of the paintings that, by their own accounts, inspired Picasso and Matisse.

—

Paul carefully recorded two of his visits to Renoir's studio, one that occurred on November 21, 1919, just before the artist died, and one on December 6, 1919, the day of his funeral.

In November he found the old painter in the studio that he had built on the edge of his property, Les Collettes, in Cagnes-sur-Mer in the south of France: "He seemed pleased to see me, and although I had a sense that he had lost weight, he was always cheerful, happy to paint, and as charming and clever as he was always said to have been . . . I brought him a photograph of a big Corot figure that I had just bought. 'Corot,' he said to me, 'is a creature apart in the nineteenth century, he is timeless.' . . .

"Before sunset, we brought Renoir back from his studio to his villa . . . he in his wheelchair, wrapped in furs and with a beret on his head. I walked beside him, bareheaded, talking to him about the beautiful spectacle of nature. The path was lined with olive trees, women picked the ripe olives, children played, dogs rested in the last rays of sunlight and the women paused to say, 'Good evening, M. Renoir'; the children stopped playing and the dogs came to greet their master. And he, like a grand priest, lowered his head and, smiling, replied, 'Good evening, good evening.'

"At that moment, through olive trees that seemed to become increasingly gnarled, the sea became bluer, the women more beautiful, the sun warmer, to cry out their admiration for the man who had known how to paint women, nature, sun."

—

Paul returned to Les Collettes only two weeks later for Renoir's funeral, after his death on December 3. He was one of the few people present at the burial of one of the greatest symbols of French art of the nineteenth and early twentieth centuries.

"His coffin rested in a modest hearse, without horses, adorned with ostrich feathers . . . The cortège set off, slowed down by a number of men, down the steep coast road that leads from Les Collettes to the little village of Cagnes. A church, really more of a simple shed, welcomed the crowd and friends from the neighborhood, with rudimentary pews, the coffin placed in front of the altar against two half doors with lowered blinds.

"The service began very simply, with no sermons, no music, no ceremonial dress, as Renoir himself would have wished. The priest, his friend, a great man, uttered the ritual prayers, but he did so with an emotion that affected the entire congregation: words of praise for the great painter, the great man of goodwill as well as the great believer who, behind his rebellious façade, always sang the beauty of nature . . . I think that in other times, other ages, he would have had a national funeral."

Apart from the story of his initiation into the business, Paul wrote very little: a preface here and there, an article in an art magazine. Besides these fragments of memoir, he felt that it was not his role or his destiny to write. Was this a result of an inability to sit still, shyness, indifference, depression, or lucidity? It is hard to know. Though Paul was keen for recognition, publishing his opinions on the theory of art did not seem a necessary part of his identity.

Nor do I have testimony of his experiences in the First World War. I haven't found any of the letters from the front that he should have written to the pretty young wife he had married in July, a month before war was declared. They were probably lost in the upheavals of 1940. Having enlisted, like all the young men of his age, in 1914, he was demobilized in 1916 for poor health, the first signs of the ulcer that was to plague him for the rest of his life. All I have of him from this period is a brittle, yellowed photograph of a soldier with a mustache like those worn by the *poilus* of times past.

There isn't much evidence of his political opinions either. Yet we do know that having been a fervent admirer of the de Gaulle of the Free French, he strenuously distanced himself from the man on May 13, 1958,* to become

---

*Translator's note: The Algiers Putsch, which led to General de Gaulle's return to power.

openly anti-Gaullist. Living in New York, he had harsh words for the arrogance of the general.*

Having lived a bourgeois life, Paul was a wise man who came from the calm left and might have been called a radical socialist. As a student he had fought the anti-Dreyfusards, and he admired the French socialist leader Jean Jaurès. In 1936 he voted for the Front Populaire, the left-wing coalition. In his own way, from within the art market itself and through his actions, he resisted the fascist ideas that were poisoning Europe. The heroism of his son in the Second Armored Division was also something with which he deeply identified.

Later I found many letters from the 1950s, including the one he wrote to my mother in 1952, in which he tells of the "mass of workers who can't make ends meet, who live in deprivation and on pitiful wages, will in due course rise up . . . Too many foreign-made luxury cars, too many overpriced restaurants. Too much poverty, too much outward luxury . . . and only charity for those who have nothing." This certainly wasn't a revolutionary diatribe, but the sentiments are clearly of the left. I am not trying to pretend that my grandfather was of the extreme left; far from it. Nor am I trying to minimize his bitterness at the time toward a France that had cast him out. But such expressions of outrage—and I've found many of them in his correspondence—testify to his personal revolt against injustice and inequality.

---

*General de Gaulle conducted a very personal and independent foreign policy, which was not always in line with the American one, especially when he removed France from NATO.

And yet Paul Rosenberg led a very comfortable life, and he certainly hadn't made his way from bohemia to the bourgeoisie and then to the Communist Party, as his friend Picasso had done. Still, he didn't judge current affairs purely in terms of his membership in the class that he lived within. *Gauche caviar*, we would now call it, "champagne socialism," a term used to mock anyone who doesn't automatically assume the dominant political opinions of his social milieu. As if a person's bank account determined his actions more than his convictions; as if the wealthy could vote only for the interests of their own.

—

Few ideological confidences are revealed in his papers, but in 1927 he did give a very strange interview about his family origins to "Feuilles volantes," a supplement of the magazine *Cahiers d'art*. The interviewer was E. Tériade, the famous art critic and publisher. Oddly, Tériade asks his questions very seriously and doesn't seem at all put off by Paul's fantastical replies, which are clearly intended satirically: "I come from a very old family lost in the mists of time. My ancestors, repelled by the mood in Palestine at that time, had wanted to sell the Tablets of the Law, but experts contested the sale. One of my ancestors authenticated the vase of Soissons . . . I find one of my ancestors among the Knights Templar. He died at the stake, and for the first time in his life he gave something away: his soul, to God . . . My father went to Mesopotamia, to examine the remains of the Tower of Babel. He visited India, Lutetia, Belleville and Montparnasse. He was a very noble man, very cultured and so generous that he saw to it that I was born on December 29, 1881, at three o'clock in the afternoon . . . At the age of 16, I entered the family firm. For starters, my father gave me copies of all the letters to archive. That task, which could have been terribly dreary, gave me a passion for invoices, and I already dreamed of the ones that I would later sign with my own name . . . My chief concern was to know whom the paintings I was to examine were by, and whether or not they were authentic. So I was obliged to find an infallible way of gathering information on those two points. For the first, I had discovered that by secretly reading the signature on the painting, I could discover the name of the painter. As to the authenticity of the canvases . . . I looked to see whether the paintings submitted to me were reproduced in catalogs or books. If that was the case, I maintained with great authority that they were entirely authentic. Even today, I behave in a similar fashion!"[2]

"What do you think about your painters?" the interviewer asks. My grandfather's response bears more than a trace of irreverence: "I am protected by every possible guarantee, and by the opinion of appeal court experts, distinguished chemists and manufacturers of canvases and frames, and I can assure you that I sell good, fault-free merchandise . . . My greatest ambition is to show in the Lépine* competition all the tricks I'm forced to come

---

*An exhibition of do-it-yourself inventions, where the most original or useful thing gets an award.

up with to convince my clients that what I'm selling are paintings."

"What do you think of your fellow dealers?" asks the unfortunate critic, undeterred.

"I hold each of them in exactly the same esteem as he holds me."

Does that mean that this Paul, whom I see as more austere than playful, more of an ascetic than a bon vivant, also had an amusing and frivolous side? In truth, I think his character tended to be more on the gloomy side, as suggested by his correspondence with Picasso, to which I shall return.

A four-page handwritten letter that Paul sent to Henri Matisse on December 2, 1939, three months after World War II had begun, adds to this portrait of a complex soul. He is writing to the painter with questions about his art. "It seems to me that you want too much out of life," Paul replies to Matisse's nostalgic letter. "What is it? A quarter of an hour of happiness, the rest all troubles, suffering and doubt! Do you want to be even more privileged than you are, do you want the heavenly gift of creating, of expressing yourself, without the pain that that entails? Everyone pays for what he has with what he doesn't have.

"Why wouldn't you doubt it? It's what gives you your strength, the expression of youth and creativity that are in your works. Don't you think that others doubt as well? . . . I am filled with doubts, I have feelings of despair like yours . . . Look at our friend Picasso, who not only doubts but is gnawed by torment . . . Are you sure that

Corot doesn't doubt just as much as Cézanne, the master of masters, the greatest of martyrs alongside Michelangelo? . . . We are all moving irrevocably toward an ideal that we will never attain, and I say we are fortunate in this because [otherwise] it would mean the end of life . . . If you knew the despair I feel at being inactive . . . you would be calmer, because you at least can take refuge in your art."[3]

We encounter this idea of being an intermediary rather than a creator several times in his correspondence. There is, for example, this letter dated December 28, 1949, again to Matisse: "If only I could create something, if God had given me that gift, I would find boundless pleasure in doing it. But alas, I must content myself with enjoying my own admiration for the creations of others, not least your own works."[4]

—

Those who knew Paul less well give a more effusive description of him.

Pierre Nahon depicts him as a "man of middle size, of meticulous elegance," "enterprising and tenacious," "pursuing audacious strategies . . . He has a rare flair, his eye is excellent, he has contacts in the best society."[5]

According to Alfred Daber, a great dealer between 1920 and 1970, as cited by Hector Feliciano, Paul's "body began to tremble like that of an impatient child when he saw a work that he craved. A trembling that subsided only when he had obtained the painting."[6]

René Gimpel gives a less flattering picture of him:

"A fox's face with too short a muzzle. Prominent, grainy cheekbones."[7] A displeasing portrait, not least because Gimpel was a friend of Marie Laurencin, who complained that Paul had treated her harshly when she asked for an advance of the pocket money she needed to settle the bill for her Chanel coats. "Stop ordering them, then!" Paul was supposed to have said to her one day when he'd had enough of her complaints, provoking a furious response.

However, having read much of their correspondence, I had a sense that even though Laurencin sometimes pleaded poverty, she adored Paul and later my mother too. Their correspondence is more than affectionate. "My darling Marie," Paul writes to her, adding, "Can I say that without seeming forward?"

The delightful, feminine paintings of Laurencin, who was loved by the poet Apollinaire, stood out in the male-dominated cubist world. They have fallen out of fashion today, as paintings for gray and pink boudoirs, but they have a grace that touches me, grace in a time of war and fragmentation. Laurencin painted gentle figures when Léger was painting his industrial structures, violent in form and color. Was Laurencin behind the times? Perhaps it was more that she was out of step with a brutal world, and that strikes me as refreshing.

Do I treat her indulgently because she painted my portrait—at my grandfather's request—when I was four years old? Sitting still like that was a form of torture for me at that age. Apparently I had the temerity to say to her, "Don't forget, my eyes are blue!" She smilingly obliged, blessing me with two luminous lavender orbs. My mother had hung this portrait in her bedroom, but I have trouble recognizing myself in this little girl with a pale pink smock dress and eyes that are unreasonably blue.

There are various descriptions of the gallery owner Rosenberg, in which he is depicted as "a shrewd dealer with good taste."[8] Certainly, his eye was legendary. In 1952 he wrote to Braque, sending him a photograph for the authentication of a painting, but he had already made up his mind: "Looking at the knife, the lemons and the ace of clubs, I think it's very unlikely that the painting's one of yours."

In 1954, when he was in poor health, he sent his son to a Parisian auction in his stead. He was interested in several paintings and wrote Alexandre a letter giving him some suggestions merely on the basis of what he had seen in the catalog: "The Renoir number 27 isn't interesting. Number 32, the Vuillard, is really a little masterpiece that you can buy. The Bonnard, number 82, not bad but a bit early. The Modigliani, number 91, I'm not sure it's authentic, as to number 95, the Renoir, stay away, it's too well known, it's been retouched and it's been on sale in all the markets in the world." All this perspicacity from an ailing old man who had examined an auction catalog.

—

It would be an understatement to say that Paul was aware of his instinct for identifying art. He could be arrogant about his gifts and about the importance of his gallery, of both the unique quality of the works shown at 21 rue La Boétie and the catalogs published under his auspices for his own exhibitions. He was especially proud to have financed the publication of two important catalogues raisonnés, one of the work of Cézanne, written by Lionel Venturi in 1936, and the other, in 1940, of Camille Pissarro's work, which was assembled by the painter's son Lucien in collaboration with Venturi.

In large part, my grandfather attributed his success to his belief that "Great paintings sell themselves." Knowing that outstanding work would be coveted by collectors, he refused to bargain when masterpieces were at stake.

Paul held his colleagues and rivals in high esteem, but not excessively so. He particularly valued Ambroise Vollard, his mentor and colleague of more than fifty years, who represented Renoir, Monet, and Pissarro and was, most important of all, the dealer and friend of Cézanne's. He gives a wonderful portrayal of Vollard in one of his letters: "You never had a sense that he was trying to sell you anything. Quite the contrary: as soon as he had mentioned the price of the painting in question, he would feel his client's lapel and ask him who had made his suit. Then he moved on to something else that had nothing to do with paintings, leaving the client to his own devices." Though Vollard was the predecessor of the great French art dealers, his gallery, on rue Laffitte in the Ninth Arrondissement, was famously shabby, crammed with dusty canvases, the only furniture a cot on which Vollard would sometimes sleep. Vollard's gallery was far from the comfort of 21 rue La Boétie.

—

At the Galerie Rosenberg, exhibitions were held year-round and lasted three weeks each. My grandfather hung the paintings himself, a sacred ceremony for any art dealer, and one to which he gave his full concentration. It was only when I saw the profusion of his catalogs that I realized the wealth of works that he'd hung over the years.

In 1962, when Paul had been dead for three years, his colleague Alfred Daber wrote to my uncle Alexandre, who had succeeded his father as head of the New York gallery: "Between 1924 and 1937, such lovely exhibitions I saw at his gallery on rue La Boétie! We sometimes talked until eight o'clock at night about subjects that seemed to have nothing to do with painting, but that painting brought us to: philosophy, metaphysics. I already wanted to correct the prevailing taste, and he told me with lucidity that it was as vain an idea as wanting to channel the waves of the sea."[9]

—

Displays of paintings by Picasso, Braque, Derain, Matisse, Léger, and Laurencin were interspersed with exhibitions by Henri Toulouse-Lautrec (1914); of French art of the nineteenth century, the preimpressionists (1917); Ingres and Cézanne (1925); Pierre Bonnard (1936); and Henri

Rousseau, known as Le Douanier, or customs officer, in 1937.

During the Great Depression, Paul returned to the nineteenth century, which was easier to sell than modern painting during those difficult economic times. In 1933 there was a Monet exhibition, and in 1934 one by Renoir. Indeed, 1936 was dazzling: Braque in January, Seurat in February, Picasso in March, Monet in April, Matisse in May, Laurencin in July.

Paul's big exhibitions of works by Picasso were always an event. The first one, in 1919—and I shall come back to it—was devoted to 160 unpublished noncubist drawings. The 1926 exhibition was one of the most imposing and was followed ten years later by a one-man show, featuring twenty-nine paintings and drawings, that attracted six hundred visitors a day, and in which Rosi (Picasso's nickname for Paul) was so excited, it was "as if the paintings had been created especially for him," observed a colleague amazed by the beauty and profusion of the works.[10]

—

Paul loaned many canvases to other institutions. For example, he contributed to the first French retrospective of Picasso's works in 1932 at the Galerie Georges Petit, but also on the other side of the Atlantic at the Wadsworth Atheneum, in Hartford, Connecticut, in 1934. Picasso was a huge draw in the art world and caused an enormous stir in the United States. Paul had insisted that the exhibition contain a verse from a fable by La Fontaine,

"The Camel and the Floating Sticks," which he then re-published in the catalog of the 1936 Paris exhibition and which he thought might open the eyes of the skeptics:

Those things we find uncanny or alarming,
Custom can make acceptable and charming;
Your earlier intense desire to flee them
Is lessened further every time you see them.

He spent months with his friend Alfred Barr selecting the works and undertaking the preparation for the first big Picasso retrospective at the Museum of Modern Art in New York and then in Chicago, at the Art Institute. That was in 1939 and 1940. Paul loaned more than thirty canvases to this exhibition, which meant these paintings had escaped the clutches of the Nazis. Barr was deeply grateful for Paul's willingness to enable this momentous show.

The other great painters of the Rosenberg "stable" fol-lowed in the aftermath of the Picasso exhibition. For in-stance, Paul devoted to Braque three major exhibitions—in 1936, 1937, 1938—and one, from April 4 to April 29, 1939, probably one of the last to be held at the Galerie Rosenberg in Paris, on the eve of the war. To complete the trio, Léger had joined the roster of artists represented at 21 rue La Boétie in 1924.

As for his "fourth musketeer," Matisse, Paul had also known him for a very long time. The correspondence be-tween Matisse and my grandfather is still the property of the painter's family, kept, like all his archives, in the house where he lived at Issy-les-Moulineaux, near Paris. The house hasn't changed since Matisse's day, but the street, formerly route de Clamart, has been renamed avenue du Général-de-Gaulle.

—

It's autumn. I push the gate open. It's cold; dead leaves are scattered on the lawn. I step inside an old-fashioned little house that makes a sharp contrast with the modernity of the conservation of the family archives. All the documents are digitized, and I'm settled at a computer by the curator, beside the radiator, in the very room that served as the painter's model for one of his most important transitional period paintings, *The Piano Lesson*,* a key canvas in the Matisse oeuvre. The double windows, the railing of the balustrade, the garden: They're all there, just as they are in the 1916 painting, giving me an immense appreciation of the artist's genius for conveying light and color.

The exchange of letters between Paul and Matisse began that same year. Their correspondence was regular and warm, apart from a few digs from Pierre Matisse, the artist's son, who thought that his father had become too dependent on Paul for representation.

In 1922 Matisse loaned Paul some canvases from his own collection, a Cézanne and a Courbet, for the Galerie Rosenberg exhibition *The Great Masters of the Nineteenth Century.* "This exhibition," my grandfather

---

*Now in the Museum of Modern Art, New York.

writes, "will also prove that the artists of our time . . . remain within the tradition, and that in their turn they honor French painting."[11] He was still obsessed with the idea of showing the through line of art, that the works that he showed and that provoked howls of outrage from the bourgeoisie were in the tradition of the art history of his country.

On December 22, 1934, Henri Matisse writes to his son Pierre that "business isn't going well. I sense a general feeling of apathy. Only Rosenberg has shown any warmth and offered me an exhibition." Two days later, in another letter to his son, Matisse confides: "I saw Rosenberg, who galvanized me, told me I was wrong to allow myself to be forgotten. He told me he had big names— the likes of Matisse and Picasso. That he wanted me to have an exhibition at his gallery, that he would put his exhibition space at my disposal . . . He showed me many beautiful paintings, van Gogh, Corot, Renoir, all new on the market. He told me how painting was everything for him, that it was the place where he lived."[12]

But things aren't always idyllic between a painter and his dealer. On January 22, 1938, again in a letter to Pierre, who was based in New York and was warning him against the exclusive deal he had made with the Galerie Rosenberg, Matisse acknowledges that he has no illusions about his dealer, even though he knows that he can't do without him: "As for Rosenberg . . . I've known him for a long time . . . Particularly when he yelled at me before signing a deal with me. I'm not with him for sentimental reasons, it's just so that I can use him . . . And then there are all the favors he has done me, and above all he knows how to glorify painting."

That was exactly what Picasso had understood in 1918, and it was likely one of the reasons that he made an extremely rare gift to Paul.

MOTHER AND CHILD

Initially it was called *Portrait de Madame Rosenberg et sa fille*. Later it appeared in various postwar catalogs, under the more American title of *Mother and Child*, before reacquiring its original name. Today it is prominently displayed in the Musée Picasso in Paris.

This portrait of my mother on my grandmother's lap was Picasso's gift to his new dealer, to mark the agreement they signed in Biarritz in 1918, even though Paul had tried to commission the piece. The painter even used the gesture to switch genres.

The painting is large, very large, and a bit academic, in the style of Ingres or Renoir but without the innate grace of those painters. It shows my grandmother sitting in an old tapestry armchair, holding my mother on her lap, a plump little doll in a white dress with blue ribbons. This painting, which scandalized the cubists, who thought that Picasso was "betraying" them, marks his return to neoclassicism.

—

I saw that painting throughout my childhood, first at my grandparents' Parisian apartment, then at my mother's. Paul attached great importance to it, and it was one of the first paintings he tried to retrieve after the war. The painting was said to have been stolen for Göring, perhaps because it reminded him of the old masters.

I used to look down on it a little, finding it too conventional, a sort of Virgin and Child on an Henri II armchair. Now I come to sit and meditate before it at the Musée Picasso, where I always thought it belonged. Since the days of André Malraux, the minister of culture under de Gaulle, the state has allowed anyone inheriting a work of art to donate it to a museum in lieu of paying a considerable inheritance tax. This measure was introduced to enrich French collections, which were poorer than many collections abroad, and to keep works that belong in national museums from being dispersed. That was what nearly happened to this family portrait: a rich Texan offered to buy the painting for a very good price, much higher than the inheritance tax that I was obliged to pay. But the idea of seeing this treasured painting leave for Houston was too painful in the end. It certainly would have distressed my mother. Fortunately, I recognized that donating it to the Musée Picasso was the right thing to do for the legacy of my family. I'm proud that the painting now adorns the walls of this Parisian institute of the arts.

In autumn 1918 the portrait was a sensation. On September 27, Paul wrote to Picasso: "Everyone knows that Picasso has painted the portrait of my wife and my daughter. Léonce heard Cocteau talking about it, and obviously he was hoping it would be cubist, even though Miche is *rondiste*."[1]

My grandmother's face is, more than the rest of her, characteristic of Picasso, in a vein that is similar to the portraits of Olga, his wife. The painting is highly valued by art historians, even though I find it rather severe. Looking at it for the hundredth time, I try to work out why Picasso gave my grandmother such a melancholic face. At the same time I wonder why my mother, who seems so vital, is made to look so plump. Might Picasso have been prefiguring his series of Giants?

Surely my grandmother would have preferred to have had her portrait painted by Giovanni Boldini, a mundane painter of the early twentieth century. Margot, who was inclined to be outspoken, admitted as much to Picasso. In response, Picasso drew a sketch in Boldini's most flattering manner, with flounces, a parasol, collars, and feathers, and sent it to my grandmother, signing it "Boldini." I'm not sure which one Margot found more gratifying in the end . . . The Picasso was stolen by the Germans but recovered just before it left for Berlin. The fake Boldini disappeared during the war, never to be seen again.

There were other family portraits by Picasso. A gouache of my mother, in a blue dress by the sea, a little girl with red cheeks and windblown hair, was painted a year after *Mother and Child*, in 1919, on the beach at Biarritz. Amazingly, this was identified by an alert collector having an anisette in a café in central France in the 1960s, who recognized it as the portrait of Mlle Rosenberg. The café owner, who had been given it during the occupation by a man in need of a sandwich, kindly returned it to my grandmother, who rewarded him handsomely.

The portrait of Paul himself, a drawing whose lines have faded since 1919, is even more touching. Paul is an elegant figure: mustache, high-buttoned shoes, and double-breasted suit. He is sitting in a relaxed pose, on an armless chair, his left arm casually resting on its back. His well-manicured right hand, holding the inevitable cigarette, rests on his knee. This little picture is drawn, like the big family portrait, in the style of Ingres, but with a particular focus on the piercing, mischievous eyes of my grandfather; very Picasso. In the words of Michael FitzGerald, it is "[a] blend of ease and sophistication . . . coupled with the intense scrutiny of [Paul's] gaze [that was] noted as his trademark."[2]

I still have the photographs of two vanished portraits of my mother, *Micheline with Rabbit* and *Micheline as a Nurse*. She must be four or five years old at the time of their creation. The drawings were done in charcoal. Stolen like the others by the Germans but never recovered, they may have gone up in smoke in the courtyard of the Musée du Jeu de Paume, in the bonfires of the occupying forces, or perhaps they were hung in a child's bedroom somewhere in Russia, or Berlin, or Paris, between the Seventh and Sixteenth Arrondissements, in the apartment of a wealthy French family that either collaborated with the Nazis or looked away from the question of the drawings' provenance.

PAUL AND PIC

That *Mother and Child* sealed a covenant, an unshakable agreement. Rosenberg and Picasso: Was theirs a story of fraternal friendship or a professional alliance? Where did it come from: this mutual fascination between the establishment dealer and the bohemian painter? What did these two men have in common: the gallery owner (accustomed to the work of Renoir and Monet) and the painter who once pronounced dealers "the enemy!" to Léonce, when he was one of Picasso's dealers between 1914 and 1918? How was it possible for Picasso and Paul to have had such a close friendship when the artist saw the artist-dealer relationship in class terms?

—

In fact, much more bound the two men than a commercial contract. Theirs was an intense collaboration and aesthetic alliance. Indeed, my grandfather was recognized as the man who had orchestrated Picasso's career, as his "impresario."[1]

More than any other artist, it was Picasso who set up the dealer not only as his spokesperson and intermediary but essentially as his agent. He had very quickly realized that if a painter were to effectively address the public, he had to have just the right dealer, someone with a deeply compatible aesthetic sensibility and nature who would thoughtfully exhibit his work and advocate for him so that the public would understand his originality, his creativity. Picasso intuitively understood the necessity of forging a deep personal bond with the person who would be identified with the exhibition of his canvases.

Paul knew how to comply with these requirements, enabling Picasso to turn his dealer into a close adviser and traveling companion. "The artist and the gallery owner made one another," Pierre Nahon later said.[2]

Picasso was born in October 1881; Paul, in December of the same year, so they were exact contemporaries. But Paul belonged to the bourgeoisie; Picasso, to the avant-garde. Picasso soon recognized, however, that he could count on Paul to sell his paintings and even though Paul sold hardly any before the mid-1920s, the artist was in a position to wait. Paul could sell the work of his impressionists while gathering support for the contemporary painters who were his passion. Picasso quickly understood that Paul would be able to make and maintain his reputation. Both men readily grasped the significance of the press and cultivated those critics or writers like Pierre Reverdy, who understood this new style of painting and knew how to bring it to the attention of the broader public. Here again a new collaboration was inaugurated among artist, dealer, and art critic.

It was Paul's mission to move Picasso from his position in the avant-garde to that of a master of modern painting, "the greatest of the twentieth century," as Michael FitzGerald was to call him.[3] Between 1918 and 1939 Pablo Picasso and Paul Rosenberg promoted each other, creating Picasso's image and definitively establishing the reputation of my grandfather's gallery.

From the outset Paul felt boundless admiration for the painter's genius. This was an enthusiasm that was all the more surprising, given that, unlike his brother, he had originally been drawn to a more classical form of painting—that of Corot, of Courbet, of the impressionists, of Cézanne and van Gogh—and had never been particularly convinced by to the vogue for cubism.

In January 1918 Picasso, in straitened financial circumstances, approached my grandfather to sell him a Renoir. But it was not until a face-to-face meeting in the summer of that year that the spark of friendship was ignited.

—

Paul called Picasso his spiritual brother, and what he felt for him was certainly something like a *coup de foudre* (love at first sight) of friendship. Indeed, something happened between them—to the extent of complicity, affection, and I would daresay fraternity.

They met at Biarritz, in the villa La Mimoseraie of Eugenia Errázuriz. This beautiful Chilean woman, a patron of the arts of the belle époque, was a leading light in the world of dealers in fine arts in the 1920s. Picasso had met her through Jean Cocteau. She was a friend of Arthur Rubinstein and Sergei Diaghilev and devoted to the Ballets Russes, probably explaining the connection with Picasso, who also had strong ties with the ballet company. It was in ballet circles that he met Olga Khokhlova, whom he later married and with whom he had a son, Paulo.

In July 1918, Eugenia invited Olga and Picasso to spend their honeymoon at her house in Biarritz. Picasso happened to be looking for a new dealer at the time. Berthe Weill's gallery had probably been the first to sell a painting by Picasso (for 150 francs) around 1901, just as she was the first to show paintings by Matisse in 1902. But Picasso soon felt that he needed the financial stability that would allow him to paint with peace of mind. Vollard, notable for discovering Cézanne, bought twenty paintings from him for 2,000 francs in 1906, but this was not enough to free Picasso from financial worry.

In 1910 Picasso charmed Kahnweiler, who became his dealer in his gallery on rue Vignon, near the Madeleine in Paris. In 1913, Picasso made his first "serious" money when Kahnweiler bought twenty-three paintings from him for 27,250 francs. This was the equivalent of $117,500 today, or just over $4,800 per canvas. Picasso had never had so much money in his life.

His sense of security didn't last long. In 1914 Kahnweiler was forced to shut down his gallery because he held German nationality. Picasso was compelled to find a new gallery.

—

Léonce Rosenberg succeeded Kahnweiler as Picasso's dealer in 1915. At the time Léonce, passionate about cubism, said to Picasso, "Together we will be invincible. You will be the creation, I the action."[4]

Léonce, who had professionally parted company with his brother in 1910, was the more adventurous of the two. More avant-garde and more of a spendthrift too, acquiring more paintings than he sold. Paul, who was more prudent by nature, betting on nineteenth-century French painters and the impressionists, made calculated incursions into the art of his contemporaries.

Paul the traditionalist and Léonce the modernist? For a long time the accepted wisdom was that Léonce was a gifted talent spotter but a terrible businessman, and Paul an astute businessman, more inclined toward business than art for its own sake. In fact, Paul wasn't very interested in old masters, unlike his colleagues who did a thriving trade in these safe bets, and instead took risks by taking on contemporary painters. Laurencin was one of the first of these, in 1913.

As late as 1943 Paul wrote, "It would be so much simpler and more lucrative for me to make exhibitions of the great French nineteenth-century masters rather than contemporary works that unsettle our visitors."[5]

Besides, in the early years of the twentieth century, dealing in Renoirs meant promoting the art of the recent past. As for the delicate masterpieces of Monet, who died in 1926, they had not yet attained the classic status they have today.

Paul wasn't interested in Jean-Honoré Fragonard or François Boucher, both then in vogue, or, unlike his brother, in Gris or Léger. Indeed, Léonce saw cubism as the culmination of all painting, much like those who saw the fall of the Berlin Wall not just as the end of a historical period but as the end of history itself.

—

In his Galerie de l'Effort Moderne on rue de La Baume not far from rue La Boétie, Léonce wanted to make Picasso the standard-bearer of a school of which the painter himself had wearied. Picasso wanted to break with artist theorists such as Albert Gleizes and Jean Metzinger and aspired to alter his style of painting. This was a time when he was distancing himself from the cubists and turning his attention instead to Diaghilev and the Ballets Russes, whose stage sets he wanted to design (much to the displeasure of Léonce, who believed that Picasso was keeping the wrong company if he wanted to fulfill his destiny as emblem of the new school of painting).

Yet Picasso was in fact returning to his roots in his Rose Period and to his harlequins, who had vanished among the pure, hard lines of cubism. He fell under the influence of Cocteau and his famous *Le Rappel à l'ordre*, in which the poet rebuked him for allowing himself to become the prisoner of other painters who had copied him and limited the scope of his art. So partly for personal reasons that marked a genuine evolution in his work, but also to attract the patronage of cultural figures such as Cocteau and Eugenia Errázuriz, Picasso began to move from cubism toward a neoclassical style.

By 1918 relations had cooled between Picasso and Léonce, and Picasso was ripe for his encounter with Paul, even though the artist had until then been Léonce's most cherished artist. I have found no trace of what must have been a fraternal crisis of conscience for Paul, a source of jealousy for Léonce, or, at the very least, the basis for heated debate between the brothers. All I have found is a statement from Léonce made much later. He was a man who knew how to make the best of things, who saw that he was going to lose his painter anyway, and who concluded that it was better if Picasso stayed in the family.

—

The meeting between Paul and Picasso took place that summer before the end of the First World War. The Rosenbergs had taken a villa in Biarritz, a few hundred yards away from the one owned by the Errázuriz family. Also nearby was Georges Wildenstein, friend and colleague. In fact, the entire Parisian art world convened at the home of Mme Errázurriz, La Mimoseraie. Eventually a verbal agreement was reached: Paul would become Picasso's representative in France and Europe, and Wildenstein would assume that role in America, where he had already established a gallery. But Wildenstein remained in the background, and when the two dealers fell out in 1932, Paul became Picasso's international representative and remained so until the end of the war. No actual contract was signed, but Paul was given *première vue*, or the right of first refusal, on Picasso's works. This was a model to which he later returned, first with Braque, then Matisse.

That summer marked a milestone in the family, for both good and ill. The positive was the freedom enjoyed by Paul and Picasso to develop their business dealings and personal friendship. The downside was the deterioration of the relationship between the Rosenberg and Wildenstein families.

From that time onward there was a very warm bond between Picasso and Paul. The painter savored the peace of mind that came from his contract with Léonce's brother; he saw the possibility of escaping the lure of cubism, which Paul wasn't so keen on. Picasso knew that if he showed his work at the Galerie Rosenberg, he wouldn't be cataloged as just another avant-garde painter but would win his place in the company of masters of the century just past.

Picasso understood early on the connections that existed between artistic creation and the marketplace, and he sought to impose careful control over the exhibition of his works. As Roland Penrose writes, "Picasso's friendship with Paul Rosenberg was increased by the dealer's usefulness as a protector of his interests and the organizer of exhibitions in his fashionable Gallery."[6]

Picasso was thrilled to find a dealer who grasped his desire to transcend cubism. Paul's genius lay in his ability to effectively juxtapose Picasso and Turner, Monet and Delacroix. But Picasso was not the only one to have been guided in that direction by his dealer. Paul took the same approach with Matisse. As for Braque, with Paul as his dealer, he moved from cubism to . . . Braque. Paul encouraged all his artists to reintroduce the subject into their painting, even in abstract works. His sense of aesthetics aligned with his commercial instincts, and time ultimately proved him right.

For the first Picasso exhibition at my grandfather's gallery, in October 1919, it was Picasso who personally paid for and designed the invitation to the opening. Both men saw this exhibition as representing a break with Picasso's previous style: there was not a single cubist work to be found among the 167 drawings and watercolors whose variety delighted visitors to the exhibition.

By selecting these particular works, both painter and gallery owner opted to display a direction for Picasso that was less radical and largely unknown to the public. Picasso had found a way of announcing his return to neo-classicism, while at the same time revealing himself to be a more open painter than was generally thought. He was essentially declaring his refusal to be pigeonholed, to be limited to the one style with which people identified him.

At 21 rue La Boétie, the public discovered a profusion of drawings of harlequins, bullfighting scenes, circuses, the Ballets Russes, open windows giving out over the sea at Saint-Raphaël, portraits and still lifes closer to the

1. My grandfather in morning jacket before the First World War

2. My uncle Alexandre "Kiki" Rosenberg, a lieutenant in the Second Armored Division, at the liberation of Paris. He served for four years under General Leclerc. After the war he succeeded my grandfather as the director of the gallery Paul Rosenberg & Co.

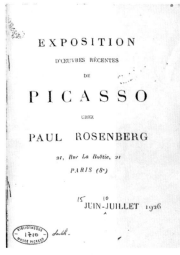

EXPOSITION

D'ŒUVRES RÉCENTES

DE

PICASSO

CHEZ

PAUL ROSENBERG

21, Rue La Boétie, 21

PARIS (8ᵉ)

JUIN-JUILLET 1926

3. The catalog of a 1926 exhibition of recent works by Picasso

4. Paul Rosenberg & Co., East Fifty-seventh Street, New York, 1941–1953

5. *Micheline en infirmière* (*Micheline as a Nurse*), a drawing of my mother by Picasso that disappeared during the Second World War and has yet to be found

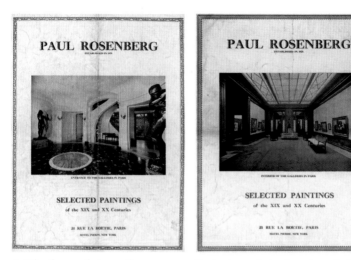

6. The foyer of the gallery on rue La Boétie, featured on the cover of a 1935 exhibition catalog

7. A view of the interior of the gallery on rue La Boétie, featured on the cover of a 1936 exhibition catalog

8. *Micheline au lapin* (*Micheline with Rabbit*), another Picasso drawing of my mother that vanished during the Second World War and has not yet been recovered

9. *Portrait de Madame Rosenberg et sa fille* (*Mother and Child*), painted by Picasso in 1918, at the Musée Picasso

10. Postcard sent by Picasso to my mother from London in 1919, when she was two years old

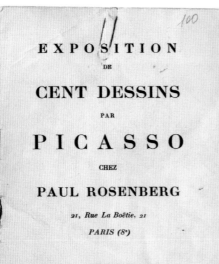

11. The catalog of a 1927 exhibition of one hundred drawings by Picasso

12. A photograph of Picasso in the 1920s, which he inscribed to my grandfather

13. The main stairway of the gallery on rue La Boétie, with paintings by Picasso and André Masson

14. The gallery on rue La Boétie during a Picasso and Marie Laurencin exhibition

15. A broken photographic plate of a 1937 Braque exhibition at rue La Boétie

19. My grandfather with a Matisse painting in the 1930s

OPPOSITE:
16. The photograph of a painting by Georges Braque that was used as a model for the design of the marble mosaics set into the floor at rue La Boétie
17. An exhibition of drawings by Matisse at rue La Boétie, June 1937
18. The Matisse exhibition of October–November 1938

20. The Institut d'Étude des Questions Juives (IEQJ, Institute for the Study of Jewish Questions) was inaugurated at 21 rue La Boétie in May 1941. This photograph shows the notoriously anti-Semitic author and guest of honor, Louis-Ferdinand Céline (left), in front of the building.

21./22. Posters advertising *The Jew and France*, an exhibition organized by the IEQJ and on view at the Palais Berlitz in 1941

23. The installation of a portrait of Marshal Pétain in the foyer of 21 rue La Boétie for the inauguration of the IEQJ

24. Céline at the IEQJ in May 1941

25. The slogan in the events hall at the IEQJ reads, "We fight against the Jew to give France back its true face: a native face"; beneath it is a poster "explaining" genetics.

26. A poster of the "Jewish bird of prey" devouring a bloodied France in the IEQJ's events hall. The paneling and glass of my grandfather's exhibition space are visible in the photograph.

27. My grandfather, in one of his favorite poses, examining a painting

28. My grandfather in New York, cigarette holder dangling from his lips, showing a magnificent Renoir to W. Somerset Maugham

29. With my grandparents Paul and Margot in the summer of 1950, when I was two years old

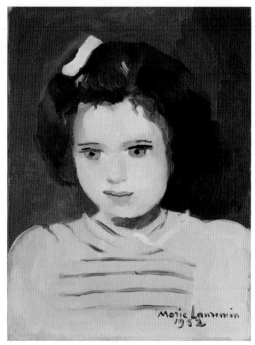

30. Marie Laurencin painted my portrait when I was four.

31. With Picasso at his farmhouse in Notre-Dame-de-Vie, near Mougins, in 1968

32. My grandfather at rest—a rare sight. This photograph was taken by my aunt Elaine in the 1950s.

33. My grandfather as he remains
in my childhood memories

34. With my
grandfather in
the early 1950s.
In his hand is an
ever-present pack
of Lucky Strikes.

classics than anything that people had known of Picasso until then.

In the autumn Paul persuaded Picasso to move to the building next door, 23 rue La Boétie, where he and Olga occupied two floors. The two men became intimate in the manner of brothers—inseparable.

—

I had a palpable sense of that intimacy when I read through a cache of 214 letters that Paul wrote to Picasso between 1918 and his death in 1959, many of them composed at the end of the First World War and continuing through 1940, when the Second World War altered the terms of their relationship.

What remains of this correspondence is accessible to researchers at the Musée Picasso. I had suspected that a trove of letters was kept in the archive there but had never taken the trouble to consult it, especially since I had so desperately wanted to make a life for myself apart from the history of my family. Once I decided to look into the past, I spent several days perched at the end of a long table in the library, on the top floor right under the rafters, with those letters before me, hoping to gain a better understanding of what it was that linked two such seemingly different men.

It's strange, this one-way correspondence, in which you're forced to imagine the absent replies, trying to fill in the blanks, to tease out the nuances of my grandfather's relationship with Picasso in those years. Apparently, Picasso didn't write much, and the few letters he did send to Paul were stolen by the occupying forces or by French colleagues during the war. Perhaps one day I'll stumble across letters to my grandfather in an old chest of drawers somewhere, ones that begin "Mon cher Rosi" and that are signed by "Pic," as my grandfather called the painter.

I am trying to reconstruct that relationship, that singular dialogue between the two men. What did they have to say to each other? Did they exchange platitudes, details about married life, or, like Johann Wolfgang von Goethe and Johann Peter Eckermann in their famous *Conversations*, did they talk about Racine and Delacroix? What is certain is that like children, they called to each other from the windows of their respective kitchens, which looked out on the same courtyard. Apparently it wasn't unusual for Picasso to hold up the painting he was currently working on so that Paul could see it through the window. And few days passed without Picasso's visiting his dealer, who already seemed a genuine friend.

These letters have the elegant slanted cursive handwriting typical of the early twentieth century. "Mon cher ami" is followed by "Mon cher Pic" or "Mon cher Casso" (as my mother called Picasso when she was a child). For Picasso, these lighthearted notes were at odds with those he received from Léonce, who was more formal in his bearing, despite his predilection for the avant-garde.

The familiar *tu*, absent for twenty years, suddenly appears with the liberation and remains throughout the 1950s, as if these two men, still almost brothers even though they were never again as close as they had once been, had decided that the turmoil of the twentieth century had swept away the polite distance of the prewar years.

—

Paul is plainly feeling his way at first, discovering the art of the painter whose greatness he senses but is still trying to grasp. "Léonce says you're a greater painter as a cubist than you are as a painter from nature . . . Am I too narrow-minded?"[7]

In the 1920s, Picasso is having a grand time in London. Paul is fascinated by Picasso's celebrity and the excitement with which he is received into British high society. Picasso becomes a member of the "ultra chic" as described by Michael FitzGerald.[8]

—

Picasso himself confirms that in London he is "seeing the beau monde," and he seems to love every minute of it. In fact, he retains his taste for the high life until his surrealist years, when he falls under the spell of his young girlfriend Marie-Thérèse Walter and locks himself away in his château at Le Boisgeloup.

—

In essence, these letters, which I read to soak up as much of this close male friendship as possible, deal with holidays, travels, when one or the other of them is away from Paris. And in fact, why would they have needed to write to each other when they lived within shouting distance, apart from the friendly little notes that you might drop off at your neighbor's house? "Can we come up and see you after dinner? Please reply through the window," Paul writes in 1918. Or in 1931, in a playful tone: "I dropped in at yours, you weren't there. I hereby summon you to my house."

Paul stays in Paris or leaves for Deauville in the summer, while Picasso—before the 1950s, the days of Brigitte Bardot and the *Nouvelle Vague,* or New Wave—discovers the Côte d'Azur, Juan-les-Pins, Antibes (later Cannes and Mougins), and settles there for several weeks to paint. He is as intoxicated as Cézanne or van Gogh by the colors and the dazzling sunlight of the south. In those sultry days of summer Le Midi is a wild world spurned by the bourgeoisie, who prefer the cooler climates and more snobbish atmosphere of Normandy.

—

Picasso, with his paint, his brushes, and his imagination, had no need to travel far to discover new worlds. In fact, he tended not to travel much at all and never set foot in the United States, despite the fact that he was celebrated there. Paul, however, was a passionate traveler; travel delighted his senses, and he wanted his wife and children to discover Europe. Europe—or rather the museums of Europe. For the Rosenberg family, there was no time for hanging around in the square, going shopping, or dancing flamenco in Spanish bars. These holidays were studious affairs that moved from the Kunsthistorisches Museum in Vienna to the Prado in Madrid and from the Accademia in Venice to the National Gallery in London. Paul adored

Italy. From Florence, in 1923, he wrote to his friend Pic, "I'm getting more and more disgusted by mediocre painting. Three painters *transcend admiration*: Corot, Cézanne, and you. The primitive painters and the old masters make me love your painting even more."

He discovered Egypt in January 1936 and was overwhelmed by the beauty of the Egyptian Museum, the Pyramids, and Luxor. "Such artists, unencumbered by the weight of convention!" he wrote. Jerusalem, on the other hand, left him cold. "I don't recognize my ancestors at all. I'd rather complain in Paris than wail like my fellow Jews by a wall." (In those years, during the British mandate period, the Wailing Wall was accessed only through a tiny alleyway, an arrangement that persisted until the Six-Day War in 1967, when the wall was wrested from Jordan.) There was no mystical revelation for Paul, no emotion at the sight of those ancient stones from the temple that had been destroyed.

My grandfather was Jewish by name, by affiliation, by tradition, but not by assertion. I have many memories of my grandmother, a very pious woman who recited her prayers in her bedroom every morning and evening and had a regular seat in the synagogue on rue de la Victoire, like the old prewar families who were referred to as Israelites. But I have no memory of a strong connection, if it ever existed, between my grandfather and Judaism. A heavy smoker (several packs a day), he made it a point of honor not to touch a cigarette on Yom Kippur, if only to emphasize that he was making more of a sacrifice than the rest of the family in terms of fasting and piety.

—

Paul and Pic obviously came from very different social backgrounds, and if Picasso had his bourgeois period— suit, waistcoat, cigar—it was during the years when he was close to Paul, geographically and socially. "My dream," he once told Léonce, is "to be rich but to live like a pauper."

The invoices from 1920 to 1921 that I found among the family papers reveal that by the standards of the day Paul offered his painters generous terms: Paul bought a large painting by Picasso for fifty thousand francs, a watercolor for twelve hundred francs, a cubist still life for twenty-four hundred francs (as early as October 1923 Picasso, having acquired a flair for business, more than doubled his prices). In 1941 Paul told *Newsweek*: "From Picasso's studio I choose the paintings I'm interested in acquiring, then we talk prices, and that's when the fun begins. We exchange harsh words but always in a friendly tone. Once I told him I'd like to bite one of his cheeks and kiss the other!"

So one of them had what the French would now call his bobo (bourgeois-bohemian) period. The other, who wasn't bohemian at all, frequented a society in Deauville, Évian, or Saint Moritz, yet constantly complained about everything, especially the rain in Normandy. He dreamed of the sun of the Midi.

—

"We're very busy here . . . meeting people we see every day in Paris." And Paul jokes to Picasso: "It's the sort of country you'd like, very cubist and full of proportions. It's also full of the French and foreigners, (1) of flirtatious and respectable women, (2) of gamblers and serious people, (3) of crooks and honest people, (4) of people who have gone to prison, and people who will, (5) of people who are enjoying themselves and others who just show their faces out of snobbery. There is, in fact, a disproportion," he adds, although it's impossible to tell in which of these categories—the amused or the snobbish—he puts himself.

—

But these jeremiads, which were not unusual as far as Paul was concerned, are a bit hypocritical because he didn't really dislike those holidays among Parisian high society. He marveled at his children's rosy cheeks and, like everyone else, stayed up late playing baccarat every night, dressed like the others in his tuxedo, while criticizing those, including his own wife, who intoxicated themselves with sybaritic pleasures during those *années dorées*, which were *années folles* for a small sector of French society.

Paul complains of being far from his paintings, which are still in Paris, and says he can't wait to get back to his gallery once summer is over. "All the top people are here," he writes to Picasso. "The higher the class of society, the lower their morals." In September 1929 he writes: "I'm coming back from Deauville. No rest, it's busier than in Paris, doing nothing useful, just parading about the place."

A year later we hear the same refrain: "It's all very phoney here. Everyone comes here to see and be seen. The children have the beach and the countryside; the parents have the casino and the car; and the men have the fillies. No shortage of them in Normandy! All snobs, us most of all, Margot loves all that. Soon everyone will be going to the Midi."

—

That little society in Deauville in the 1920s was a privileged one, consisting of the partygoers and socialites who later flocked to Saint-Tropez or the fashionable islands of the Antilles.

"The exhibition of the artist by the name of Picasso is announced with great fanfare for the 14th February next," Paul tells Picasso in their typically jocular tone. But in January 1921 he reminds his friend of "my harlequins, my harlequins, my harlequins!" as he is clearly concerned that the artist has fallen behind. Similar concerns are sounded in August 1929, and one feels Paul's mounting frustration. "You left without delivering my harlequin, you're terrible!" he says. For Paul, who is meticulous in his business dealings almost to the point of mania, Picasso's casual approach to his commitments is maddening.

Paul also writes, "I have not yet seen your new style," not in the tone of a fashion designer's backer asking for photographs of his latest collection but in that of a child who thinks somebody's hidden his new toy. He is thrilled by the painter's genius, as the painter is well aware.

"Your trip to Russia is the talk of the town," he writes to Picasso, who has gone to Moscow to meet Stalin and his henchmen. "I can't wait to see your 1926 production . . . Give me a vision of the 'new Picasso.'" Paul understood that Picasso's paintings would change almost year to year.

Occasionally, as on July 13, 1921, Paul issues orders that sound a bit brusque: "I need a large number of canvases for this winter. I'm ordering 100 from you, to be delivered at the end of the summer." It's odd to hear Paul talking like the manager of a retail store, placing his orders with the wholesaler on the corner.

Often, in his correspondence with Picasso and later with Matisse, he expresses his regret at being only the intermediary, never the creator. Paul knew very well that he was addressing a monumental figure of contemporary art, even as he urged him to produce new work (just as Durand-Ruel did with "his" impressionists). What fascinated Paul was the process of artistic development, which Picasso must have appreciated. Between 1918 and 1932 all of Picasso's major works passed through Paul's hands.

In the 1920s Paul told visitors to his gallery who were intrigued by these paintings, so different from anything they were familiar with, about "my dear friend Picasso, whom I look upon as a brother and whom I have known since 1906," as he puts it in his 1941 article in *Art in Australia*: "Picasso always goes beyond the boundaries; he is the greatest painter of the present day, and I am always delighted by each new series of his." He adds: "It was he,

Picasso, who overthrew past conventions and at his whim created others, and who, bored at seeing the same forms reproduced, devised his own . . . He has opened new horizons to us, and has brought painting to its only goal: '*to be works of art*,' not mere decorative creations."

—

Back in Paris, the social whirl at rue La Boétie continued apace. In 1929 Paul bought some racehorses. Was he keeping up with the Wildensteins? "I've got ten horses," he writes to Picasso. "I'm going to name them after my painters. And if a horse with the name of Picasso wins, it'll be excellent publicity for your work," he jokes, while complaining about the expense of the horses.

The same year Paul was made a member of the Légion d'Honneur. When Picasso congratulates him, Paul replies: "My dear Picasso, the chevalier thanks you for your congratulations; they've brought me one more autograph." That didn't stop him, in the same letter, from discussing his friend's current domestic and financial affairs, for which he himself assumed responsibility, and the canvases he was impatiently awaiting: "Your bills are paid . . . But you don't talk about your painting, or about what you've done, what new genre you've adopted. Your Dinard Stations of the Cross alarm me. You are massacring humanity so violently that I worry you'll do still worse damage by giving your characters a human face." Picasso's paintings of the 1930s already bear the early signs of his own internal turmoil and that of the world, as in the portraits of Dora Maar, which are distorted by the master's genius, and paintings that evoke the approaching civil war in Spain.

—

In 1927 the Rosenbergs started "taking the waters" in Vittel or Évian, to treat Paul's fragile health, his frequent attacks of ulcers. "No stress, just a calm, tranquil life. It's a dream, except for my wife, who isn't really enjoying herself. She wants to go to Deauville. I'll agree, for a bit of peace," he writes to Picasso.

What remains surprising about these letters from between the wars is the extent to which references to contemporary events in Europe are absent. It is as if the two men wanted to immerse themselves entirely in art and friendship, far from the affairs of the real world. Only the signing of the Treaty of Versailles after the First World War and the celebrations that followed are talked about with some emotion. But the stock market crash of 1929, the far-right leagues of the 1930s, the Popular Front, the Spanish Civil War, Hitler's coming to power: none of these things is mentioned in these letters, even though the correspondence spans more than forty years. Probably such matters were mentioned in conversation. In their writings, however, it's painting, always painting, and the daily concerns of a life shared by friends.

—

At times Paul seems the neglected friend who requires attention; he demands a letter or some news at the very least. The tone is affectionate, deferential, and intimate, even tender: "I haven't seen you for a week. I'm getting worried, and my friendship with you is suffering." There is something intense and exclusive about this friendship, almost as if Picasso were his only friend. Was Picasso perhaps the only one who understood his inner being? "I see your closed shutters, it's sad," Paul writes to his dear friend. "Your paintings are on my walls and I miss your daily visits." There is a sense of brotherhood not unlike that shared by the great essayist Michel de Montaigne and his friend Étienne de la Boétie.

Then come the laments about the ceaseless work needed to modernize the Galerie Rosenberg, the sluggish art market, the scarcity of collectors, and the shortage of art lovers: "I've spent a fortune on antique frames. But paintings are getting so rare that it's the frames I'm going to sell. The sauce will help people swallow the roast!" And yet, in spite of his grievances, there were splendid times when "the paintings, a real stock exchange," soared in value, toward the end of the 1920s in France or immediately after the First World War in the United States. But to listen to Paul, business was dreadful throughout his career as an art dealer.

My grandfather was prone to depression, often related to his poor health and his chronic stomach troubles. This must have been what gave him that thin, almost gaunt look that struck me even when I was a little girl. My grandmother was all plump and gentle, her ample bosom perfect for childhood cuddles.

In September 1929 Paul confides in Picasso: "My hell

must lie within, if I feel fine only wherever I happen not to be." Such a marvelous phrase. It's rare to read Paul's divulging anything about his state of mind or his private life. For instance, there were disagreements between him and my grandmother that strained their relationship. In Paul's correspondence with Picasso, however, I never found a single word on these stormy and violent episodes, despite what family members told me in confidence.

Had he ever opened up to his next-door neighbor? Perhaps it wasn't in the spirit of the times, because Paul makes no further allusions to Picasso's separation from Olga (although at the painter's request he drew up the inventory for the divorce) or to the various companions who passed in and out of his life: Marie-Thérèse Walter, most often hidden away in Le Boisgeloup, Dora Maar, Françoise Gilot, or Jacqueline Roque, who became his wife only after my grandfather's death.

—

Yet there are some genuine surprises; Paul sometimes allows himself to doodle shamelessly. My grandmother has no hesitation in doing the same. With her penholder (until she died in 1968, I never saw her write with anything but a Sergent-Major quill pen dipped into a big inkwell) she would try to draw the view from her bedroom in Deauville, most often ending up with a bunch of scribbles.

It must have been around this time that the painter drew an open window for Paul to use as an ex libris, that personal seal affixed to the first page of his books, which was used for both the Galerie Rosenberg's publications and its business cards until the death of my uncle Alexandre.

At times Paul and Picasso seem like mischievous adolescents. One of the letters from my grandfather to Picasso, dated July 4, 1919, is edged in black, the border hand drawn with a shaky pencil to convey mourning. My grandfather offered his most sincere condolences. "The parrot is dead," he writes (deliberately echoing the *petit chat* in Molière's *L'École des femmes*). This was Paul's announcement of the sad demise of the bird that Picasso had kept at the Rosenberg house, whose final moments Paul so liked to describe. And this followed immediately by "I've sold the Renoir you liked so much, *Woman Taking Off Her Blouse*," which put the gravity of the death announcement in context.

Boyish jokes, intimacies, even teasing erupt. "My dear quitter" Paul says to him, "I'm going to throw myself into painting, I'm jealous of your light. But what style should I adopt? Cubist, rondiste, loyalist, royalist, republican and monarchist? In fact I want to be a *brushist*."

Through all those years of complicity, they mix business, friendship, and favors: Paul takes charge of the practical side of Picasso's life: he orders him sheets of plywood that he needs for his collages or sells him packets of tobacco. Picasso, in turn, sends Paul sweets, which he loves, from Vogade, a confectioner in Nice celebrated for almost a hundred years. "Thank you for the beautiful fatma, the beautiful Negro, your picture and candies," writes Paul, thanking him also for his battered canvases and chocolate truffles.

And when Picasso is in London, Paul sends him off on a reconnaissance mission: "There's going to be an exhibition with two Daumiers, a Degas, a Monet. Can you tell me if it's worth me crossing the sea to go to it?"

My grandfather even gets into technical details with Picasso: "Can you paint with English pigment and brushes, on English canvas? Don't use *taffeta*, it curls when it gets wet."

—

Paul never missed an opportunity to promote his painter and friend, introducing the younger painter's work, for example, to the seventy-eight-year-old Renoir. "Saw Renoir. Told him about you. He was amazed by some things. And even more shocked by others." Picasso was thrilled by the fact that his revered master should be interested in his work. In fact, during those years he seemed engaged in a kind of painterly dialogue with Renoir that would mark his style throughout the early twenties.

Paul also liked to assert himself in his friend's eyes as the expert with the infallible eye, whose business sense never interfered with his artistic vision. "I had a visit from someone who thought he had a real one and a fake," he writes Picasso. "I reassured him by telling him they were both by you." But Paul remained oddly old-fashioned in his response to the representations of sexuality in Picasso's painting, and God knows there were plenty of those! (Pierre Daix, one of Picasso's biographers, went so far as to call Paul prudish.) Apparently,

Paul rejected the most graphic works, including a nude of Marie-Thérèse of which Paul was supposed to have said, "I refuse to have assholes in my gallery!"[9]

—

Yet for all their closeness, the relationship cools. Picasso becomes detached and increasingly involved with the surrealists from whom Paul, like Kahnweiler, maintains a distance, and their neighborly complicity gently turns into a more conventional commercial association. Paul, ever sensitive, realizes this, calling Picasso his invisible friend. It must also be noted that by the early 1930s, Picasso is spending less time on rue La Boétie and more in his residence at Le Boisgeloup, forty miles northwest of Paris, with Marie-Thérèse, the lover with whom he would have a daughter and who would inspire some of his most important works. This is a new Picasso, "lord of Bois Jaloux," as my grandfather writes to him, seeing the chasm open up between him and his friend.

After the Second World War and four years of silence, it will be even more difficult to regain their former closeness. The infrequent letters between them are no longer handwritten but typed, particularly after my grandfather suffers a stroke that keeps him from writing, and indeed from talking. However, in August 1944, when postal deliveries resume after the liberation of Paris, he warmly confesses: "There's no point telling you how much I have missed you during my exile."

It is then that the two men start addressing each other with the familiar *tu*, probably after they meet when Paul returns to Paris in 1945, to assess the state of his looted property and resume his former life. And once again, they renew their relationship with its curious blend of business and friendship, even though Picasso is no longer my grandfather's client.

Picasso has returned to Kahnweiler, his dealer before the First World War. "My dear Picasso, I can tell you that I have landed on my feet in New York. How much would you charge me for the little still life with the fruit bowl on the right and the bunch of cherries? Je t'embrasse, Paul."

On July 15, 1947, my grandfather expresses to Picasso his irritation over an attempted breach of copyright: "I'm learning right now that somebody in New York is about to produce some fabrics in 'Picasso gray.' It's illegal to use a name as famous as yours to launch any kind of merchandise. A parfumeur took Renoir's name, and after a case brought by the family they had to change the name. Will you give me the legal power to represent and defend you?"

What would Paul have said at the sight of the ubiquitous Citroën Xsara Picassos being driven around the streets of all the cities in France?

Between 1945 and his death in 1959, Paul would see Picasso only once a year at La Californie, his residence in Cannes. The days of calling from one window to the next were over.

—

It had to have been painful for my grandfather when Picasso resumed his business relations—interrupted in

1914—with Daniel-Henry Kahnweiler, who remained his dealer until the painter's death in 1973. But Paul was in New York at the time, and he was often ill. Picasso, who had drifted further away from his former dealer with every war, now returned to one of his first admirers from the early years of the century.

But my grandfather's passion for this extraordinary artist remained unbounded. "The greatest artist in the world today," he said in the 1930s. "The most prolific painter in history," he affirmed in the 1950s.

My grandmother and then my mother kept the connection alive with a few letters and visits first to La Californie, then to the farmhouse in Notre-Dame-de-Vie, near Mougins, which I remember.

My first memories of Picasso are from a long time ago. He is wearing his striped sailor's jersey, the one handed down to posterity in Robert Doisneau's famous photograph, in a restaurant in Saint-Tropez, to which he invited my grandparents and me in the 1950s, one of those lunches that seem interminable to children, and at which the *patronne* scurried over to collect the pieces of paper tablecloth that Picasso had scribbled on.

I went often with my parents to his house in Mougins, though I surely would have preferred an outing with my cousins on the beach at Cannes. The ritual was always the same. The electronic gate opened; these were the days of Jacques Tati's films, and the gadget seemed to me the height of modernity. Jacqueline in her capris and colorful blouse welcomed us outside the house. She was a woman filled with admiration of, devotion to, and love for the great man who was her husband. I can still envision her after Picasso's death, when we visited her each year, always in the same place. I remember her as a somewhat haughty widow with Spanish posture—straight as a statue—and the long neck whom Picasso painted so often, either bareheaded or wearing a scarf, turban, or mantilla.

I wasn't old enough to appreciate, let alone be amazed by, the paint-spattered parquet or the incredible disarray in the house, which at the time merely struck me as untidy. Picasso's room was in absolute shambles, and I couldn't understand how my mother, meticulous as she was, could swoon over such chaos. In his bedroom a recent canvas was used for a headboard, its face to the wall, so that the pillows would not rest against the paint.

Most of the time I ran about in the garden with Catherine, Jacqueline's daughter, or Claude, the son of Picasso and Françoise Gilot, climbing their famous bronze oak. In those days I didn't care for its neighbor in the garden, the bronze statue of *Little Girl Skipping*, a sculpture that was somehow less accessible than the oak tree. As a little girl, assuming that the child must be suffering some kind of infirmity, I was unsettled by the one shoe turned inward.

Back in the 1960s Évian bottles were made of glass and sealed with little metal caps. At the Picasso house, there was one glass case in particular that enchanted me, a curiosity that was, for once, accessible to children: it contained dozens of those little Évian caps, tortured and transformed into magical or monstrous animals by a man who could reinvent a set of bicycle handlebars, an old rake, or a bottle stopper into a work of art.

I must confess that I sometimes thought—like those back in 1920 who had criticized my grandfather for exhibiting scribbles "that a four-year-old could have done"— that too much of a fuss was made over the slightest creative gesture of Picasso. The lack of comprehension and skepticism of the prewar years was over, making way for unconditional admiration for contemporary art in general and for Picasso in particular.

—

And now more recent images come to me, of Picasso in his last years, once he had stopped leaving the house: his blue-and-white-checked peacoat; his powerful, intimidating gaze; his Spanish-inflected French, which was excellent; his approximate spelling; and especially his affection for my mother.

One day when my parents had taken me along after a hiatus of a few years, he noticed that I was growing up. "I'm going to paint your daughter," he told my delighted mother. "I see eyes all over her face!" "No!" I squealed, fleeing in terror, imagining a face that would have been distorted like the one he had painted of Dora Maar and his wartime paintings, which have never been my favorites. A fourteen-year-old girl isn't necessarily going to understand such a harsh artistic style. For me at the time, "that guy" Picasso was more of a predator of faces than a towering figure of the twentieth century. Would he have carried on if I hadn't run away? Probably not. At least I still have a photograph of myself at the age of eighteen, standing next to him, leaning against the walls of his villa. And I love his expression in that now-fading photograph: it is intensely magnetic, much like the gaze he gave himself in his earliest self-portraits in the 1900s, when he was already probing the deepest mysteries of the soul.

BOULEVARD MAGENTA

Number 1 place de la République. I was following the route of the demonstrations against the National Front. On May 1, 2002, there were still several hundred thousand of us jammed outside that door, hour after hour, so dense was the crowd that had come to protest the danger represented by Jean-Marie Le Pen, the far-right candidate for president, who had moved into the second round of the election behind Jacques Chirac. It was hot, we were anxious and thirsty, and I was, at that point, more interested in getting hold of bottles of water than in making a family pilgrimage. So I looked at the building without quite seeing it. That heavy, pompous Baron Haussmann–style edifice.

It was the building where my grandmother had lived as a girl. Margot Loévi got engaged in that building and left it on the morning of July 7, 1914, to become Mme Paul Rosenberg. (My great-grandfather Loévi, the father of Margot, her brother, Michel, and her sisters, Marianne and Madeleine, was a wine trader.) I don't think the family knew the first thing about art, modern or otherwise. And I don't know who introduced this old Alsatian family to the Rosenbergs, newly arrived from Bratislava. But for my great-grandfather, the important thing in the end was to let his daughter marry a businessman like himself, no matter that he sold canvases covered with daubs of paint rather than bottles of fermented grape juice. Apparently the entire family was fine with this, and my grandmother's dowry was generous. My cupboards are still full of her monogrammed tablecloths and sheets that have never been used and are slowly turning to dust.

Paul courted her for several months. My grandmother was a beautiful girl, and my grandfather was smitten with her. Twice a week he sent flowers from Moreux, the opulent florist's shop in the Sixteenth Arrondissement, which remained on the corner of the place Victor-Hugo until only a few years ago.

—

He talked endlessly about painting to my grandmother, who, according to family lore, knew nothing about it. I can just imagine Paul, hoping to dazzle her, boasting about a painting he'd bought, and hoping to show her a famous van Gogh from the series showing the town hall of Auvers-sur-Oise. And I imagine my grandmother, a naive, sheltered young girl, going home and asking, "'My green curtains,' 'my green curtains,' why is this young man always going on about 'green curtains'?" She would not have realized that in French, "my green curtains" (*mes rideaux verts*) and *Mairie d'Auvers* sound virtually identical.

—

As a young woman Margot had a pretty voice and was a lover of opera and operettas. She was the first to take me to see *The Merry Widow*, *La Belle Hélène*, and *Faust*, passing on to me her love of song, of the human voice, whether by Franz Lehár, Jacques Offenbach, or Charles Gounod. When I was ten, she took me for the first time to the traditional opera house in Paris, the Palais Garnier, and I was impressed by the majesty of the building, with golden ornaments on the façade and the impressive staircase, where I could imagine Maria Callas, whom I admired and still cherish, sweeping down in evening dress, followed by countless admirers and photographers . . . A dream for a little girl.

She had been cheerful and outgoing at the time of their marriage, but later she became depressive and lethargic. When my father started criticizing people who complained about their lot, aiming his ire first at his mother-in-law, then at my mother, he would say, "That's the Loévi side of the family," contrasting it with the philosophy of his own mother, Marguerite Schwartz, an exceptional woman, whose motto was to "button up"—in French, literally to grit your teeth and get on with it. In the Loévi household, you didn't button up in the face of adversity; you complained a lot and wallowed in your misfortune.

—

For me, on the other hand, Margot Rosenberg was what the French call a *grand-mère gâteau*. Not just because every walk I took with her ended with a stop at the pastry shop. Nor because I had only to mention my desire for a book, a record, or a four-color pen of the kind I'd craved for several months during the 1960s, only to be given them the following day. But also because she embodied the warm, generous bosom against which a child's sorrows were swiftly comforted. She indulged my every whim, and sleeping at her house allowed me to escape my mother's watchful eye. For me she was a very sweet old lady, and I was her cosseted granddaughter. Like my cousins, the daughters of her beloved son, Alexandre, I was spoiled rotten. And as the eldest I had all the advantages.

My grandmother spent six months of the year in New York and six months in Paris from the end of the Second World War until her death in 1968. Very stylish, she was always concerned with her wardrobe, never went out without makeup, wore hats with little veils, which I found mysterious, like a movie star of the thirties, and long black suede gloves, even in the summer, because she believed a woman couldn't go out bareheaded or gloveless, even in the sixties. She was a very comme il faut woman, whom I liked to shock with the slang that we spoke at school. Her favorite pastime was meticulously keeping her domestic account books in ink, with her big, regular, sloping handwriting. She also wrote every day to whichever of her children happened to be on the other side of the Atlantic. Each and every morning when my grandmother was in America, the postman delivered to her a sky-blue envelope bordered with red, which became her daily reading matter. I found many of these letters, numbered one to one thousand, crammed into the shoe boxes I recovered from the furniture warehouse where my mother's things were stored after her death. My grandmother's letters were full of trivia, of mundane preoccupations, as well as a few words of loneliness and of admiration for her three granddaughters, whom she adored. And so many ellipses standing in for sighs and despondency.

She never went out in the evening, had few friends, and mostly spent money on household staff: maids, cooks, chauffeurs. She didn't require this lifestyle, but she'd gotten used to it as my grandfather became increasingly successful. I remember that while my grandfather was still alive, she would ask him for a few francs before setting off to the kitchen to arrange the meals for the following day. I was aware of Paul's irritation as he reached into his pocket for such tedious expenses. If I wasn't consciously aware of the humiliation that she must have felt as she stretched her hand out toward the man with the wallet who, each evening, protested, I at least understood that a woman should try not to be dependent on her husband and that my grandmother would have been better off working. But it was not the way of her generation.

Morning and evening she said her prayers in her bedroom, far from the synagogue that she attended on Friday evenings. If you risked visiting her during the morning or late afternoon, she would lift her head from her prayer book, delighted by the family visits that penetrated her solitude. Religious practices aside, my mother was very much like her. She too was lonely throughout her life, which was punctuated—after my father's death—only by my daily visits or by the arrival of my children when they were home from school.

My grandmother didn't eat pork or shellfish and might have memorized a few words of Yiddish, yet she didn't speak or read Hebrew. She had her seat, which her mother and her grandmother had occupied, in the synagogue on the rue de la Victoire, where the cantor, the young and charming M. Adolphe Attia, was showered with compliments for his golden voice when he chanted the Sabbath prayers.

She was, like my grandfather, the epitome of those prewar Jewish families that were known in France as Israelites until the 1960s: people of Jewish descent, more or less observant, but deeply assimilated into French society, even after the horrors of the 1940s.

—

That was how I had always thought of my grandmother, who died in July 1968, at least until April 2010, when I opened those shoe boxes in the warehouses at Gennevilliers. Since then I've had a terrible time reconciling my memory of my grandmother with what I found.

Apparently she had had an affair with a man who was one of my grandfather's major competitors in the art world, Georges Wildenstein, who (as I have said) for a time was Paul's business associate. I remembered how it was decided in 1918 that Paul would represent Picasso in France and Europe and Wildenstein would represent him in America. I had never understood why the association collapsed in 1932, when Paul became the artist's sole representative. Or why it was taboo to utter the name of this family in ours.

But then one suddenly unearths artifacts from the realm of the unspoken, tucked away at the back of a chest of drawers. Do we pass over these secrets in silence? There's nothing shameful about them, even though they must have been painful at the time. Why reveal them now? They have nothing to do with anybody, except the protagonists, who died so long ago . . . I loathe absolute transparency, finding it voyeuristic at best and a bit totalitarian at worst.

But these letters provide a better understanding of my grandfather's psychology, which was skeptical and suspicious, and of my grandmother's personality, which became so withdrawn, in total retreat from the social world.

I feel unmoored in the face of such intimacy, and I turn the letters around in my hands, trying to work out what to do.

—

For my grandparents, it was a family crisis. For their children, my mother, my uncle, it was a secret shame (my mother never talked to me about it before her death) much like an open wound. My mother, at the age of fifteen or sixteen, in 1932 or 1933, was sent off to spend a few weeks with my grandmother's youngest sister, Marianne, and her husband and children, while Alexandre, who was only eleven, went to stay with my grandmother's other sister, Madeleine. The atmosphere at rue La Boétie must have been very tense. The servants, the family, their

Parisian milieu: everyone must have known, and that open secret must have been the talk of every prewar Deauville soirée.

—

I'm still pacing, clutching those letters as if I'd stumbled upon a written piece of the Kabbalah that could singe my fingers if I were ever to hide it again, leaving me with a curse lasting seven generations.

I wouldn't even have mentioned this affair if I hadn't also discovered, in the boxes recovered from the depository, a poignant document written by my grandfather in 1942, when Alexandre was fighting with Philippe Leclerc's army in Africa, sometime between the battles of Bir Hakeim and El Alamein. Paul had planned to visit his son, whom he missed terribly, but he abandoned the idea at the last minute in the face of such a difficult journey and the risk of being shot down by the Germans. It was in this period that he filled a ten-page letter with his delicate handwriting and tucked it away in the drawer of an office on Fifty-seventh Street in New York. The desk went with him to his gallery on Seventy-ninth Street, but the drawer remained locked. A few months after my grandfather's death, Alexandre, while sorting through his father's papers, happened upon this document, typed it out to make it more legible, and sent it to my mother—my grandmother had just arrived for one of her extended stays in Paris.

"You will weep as I did when you read this letter," Alexandre writes his sister. "We have understood our father even less than we thought . . . I think that in any event you will have to show this letter to our mother." Did my mother do this? Something tells me she did not. It would be better to assume that my grandmother Margot died peacefully in Paris, in 1968, a few weeks after the May *événements*.

Because the letter is harsh, very harsh. Written by Paul, it was intended to be read posthumously, as indeed it was. The letter was addressed to his wife and daughter—"his two darlings"—and the son he had been preparing to visit in Africa. It is a meditation on life, his life, on what he wanted for his family, and on the pain he felt over not having brought happiness to his beloved wife.

"My own youth was not as happy as my children's," he begins. "But when I met you, my dear Margot, I hoped I might at last hold that happiness in my hand. I thought I had found in you the companion I would cherish, the one for whom I would do anything at all to make your life more beautiful."

It seems that Margot's disappointment dated back to the First World War, which broke out immediately after her wedding in July 1914. Paul, old enough to be conscripted, was sent to the front, causing them to miss out on the first carefree years that a young couple should enjoy. He goes on at length about his nerves, his desire to establish himself, and his need to earn a living in order to keep his family in comfort. "Alas, the more I worked, the more money I made, the more I became a slave to business, a slave in chains, a Sisyphus with his rock," he writes.

He had always been financially prudent by temperament. But his anxiety about keeping up with his wife's expensive tastes was palpable. Right before her eyes she had the model of the Wildenstein family, whose lavish lifestyle must have dazzled her, though the life she led with my grandfather was certainly luxurious by any measure.

—

Then, in that letter that overwhelmed me, as if I had opened a door that should have stayed firmly shut, out came the rancor and jealousy that remained an undercurrent, a constant presence in the ensuing years. "Sadly, you didn't give me time to put a roof on my building, before the evil words of a serpent were whispered in your ears. They distorted, ridiculed my every deed," my grandfather writes in bitter, biblical terms. "I have much to reproach myself for. I should have spent less time on my business and devoted myself more to you . . . Life became torture for me in 1923, I loved you with all my heart and felt that I was losing you. Alas, you were given empty promises for the future the better to seduce you, promises that never came true, but that you thought were real, as if happiness didn't lie in the devotion of a *close* family."

Paul had come from a family that was doubtless filled with the anxieties of Jews from Mitteleuropa. His wife, who had been integrated into French society for a longer time, was more playful and carefree; she needed love, and mostly what she got was money. How could anyone have imagined that the "devotion of a *close* family" would have satisfied a woman in 1930? Meanwhile, her suitor dazzled her with a vision of the high life, the flashiness of a society that, as we know, was dancing toward the abyss in the interwar years. And yet Paul, a pessimist by temperament, gloomy by nature, was already on that brink.

"You were beautiful, everyone found you amusing, you were wooed and desired by many men, and while thinking that you were making yourself happy, you made us both unhappy . . . Your sarcasm, relying on a so-called protector, about whom I hope my son will one day ask for an explanation, your way of saying 'too late' when I declared my love to you, darkened my character, and I had to seek consolation and oblivion in work, as indeed I continue to do," he writes in his own defense.

Apparently, my grandmother got bored with the marriage. Perhaps she was frivolous, responsive only to surface and luxury. That's what seems to underlie my grandfather's thinking.

"I want to tell you all this on the eve of my departure so that you know, my dear Margot, that your ambition for wealth was a desire for appearance, for possession. As for me, my sole desire was to make you happy (the children and you), and assure you that I would grant you all a secure future that would enable your independence. No, Margot, I can't rebuke you anymore. Time masks all wounds, but my own still bleed with the loss of my happiness. In order that your heart may cease to suffer, that posthumous remorse may not be too much of an affliction, I shall shoulder some responsibility myself. My own character, I confess, is very self-contained, and I should have liked to find in you a less skeptical person, someone more profound, with whom I could have exchanged ideas, shared my aspirations, and talked about something other than trivial matters. And if at root your being is devoted solely to goodness, then your spirit and your mind are incompatible with the needs of a serious, loving and devoted man."

I don't believe my grandmother was ever aware of this letter with its very accusatory, self-justifying language and tone. I very much hope that is so.

She wanted a divorce, but my grandfather was adamantly opposed to the idea. Since, according to their marriage contract, all property was held jointly, I suspect that love and rage were not the only reasons for his refusal to divorce. From the moment Margot gave up her life as Wildenstein's lover and sacrificed her life as a woman, she punished Paul by relinquishing all interest in his social and professional world; by refusing to do any of the things that might, in my grandfather's eyes, have been expected of the wife of a major Parisian art dealer.

—

Sixty years later, and the Wildenstein name pops back into the public eye. I'm skimming one of the newspaper stories in which you never know what's true and what's made up, gossip about inheritance scandals, unscrupulous art evaluations, or suspect fiscal investigations of them. The French have little sympathy for people with vast fortunes, and there can be no doubt that this family of prosperous art dealers falls into this category. Although it's also possible that malice dictates what the papers say.

On the other hand, I remember a story from about ten years ago, when the Wildenstein family brought a case against Hector Feliciano, the author of *The Lost Museum*. He was said to have defamed them by claiming that Georges Wildenstein, my grandmother's alleged lover, had done deals with the Nazis. That was what suddenly prompted me to seek out the details of the case when my own family's private history came to light.

The trial took place in 1999. The Wildenstein family was furious: "What could be more horrible for the members of a Jewish family than to find themselves implicated in an act of betrayal, of collusion with the German occupiers against France!" . . . "The Wildensteins loved France so much that even then they didn't buy German cars," their lawyer, Maître Chartier, declared. This is a curious response, one that negates sixty years of Franco-German reconciliation and throws history back in the faces of the Germans who are so dedicated to consigning it to oblivion. But in the end, I'm more concerned with the family-related intrigues of the past than with the German cars of today.

The Georges Wildenstein Gallery was actually run during the war by a certain Roger Dequoy. This is where the stories diverge. According to the Wildenstein family, Georges had severed all communication with his former employee, who was going so far as to disparage him in letters that he, Dequoy, sent to the General Commissariat for Jewish Questions. As far as the family was concerned, Dequoy's assertions were false and malicious.

According to Antoine Comte, the prosecution lawyer, Dequoy acted as an intermediary between Wildenstein and the German authorities. As evidence for this he cited a meeting in November 1940 in Aix-en-Provence among George Wildenstein, his employee Dequoy, and Hitler's art dealer, Karl Haberstock. In the course of this conversation, Comte claimed, an agreement was reached: Wildenstein recovered some of his confiscated property and was able to reopen his gallery under Dequoy's name; in exchange, Dequoy is said to have agreed to work for the Nazis.

A serious accusation but one that, according to the prosecutor, was based on papers in the American archives of the Office of Strategic Services (OSS, later the CIA), which were declassified in 1998 and were said to contain a special report on the Wildenstein Gallery that had been compiled in 1945. The existence of both the agreement and the OSS report is confirmed by Lynn Nicholas in her book *The Rape of Europa*: "In November [Haberstock] and Dequoy went to Aix, where they met Wildenstein and came to certain agreements . . . It was proposed that Wildenstein would exchange 'acceptable' pictures from his stock for the modern works so unacceptable to the Nazis, which Haberstock would send to him in the United States. Wildenstein would sell them through the New York branch of his firm."

Initially, the Wildensteins were denied the six million francs in damages and interest that Alec and Guy

Wildenstein, Georges's grandsons, had demanded for the assault on their grandfather's memory, which resulted in the family's decision to appeal the case.

After the court of appeal refused to overturn the initial judgment, the daily newspaper *Libération*, quoting the court's final statement, said that Georges Wildenstein "can legitimately be presented as one of those individuals who on the one hand cultivated 'ambiguity,' both as a 'victim of the looting of the occupying forces,' and on the other, 'in parallel pursued, via an intermediary, operations on the Parisian art market' under the occupation.

"In the court's opinion, 'the allegations of contacts with the Nazis by Georges Wildenstein cannot be called manifestly erroneous' since it is established that Wildenstein 'had, before the war, entered into a business relationship with Karl Haberstock, who was known to be one of the Führer's artistic advisers and a high-ranking Nazi. During the occupation, Haberstock acted as a protector of Roger Dequoy . . . who was running the gallery in Paris at the time, and who 'one may imagine was keeping up relations with Georges Wildenstein,' in exile in New York. There is 'much evidence to suggest' that the famous art dealer, whose collection had been partly looted by the Germans, 'maintained business contacts with the occupying forces.' "[1]

This ruling, disobliging at the very least, led the Wildensteins to appeal once more in the Cour de Cassation, which is supposed to judge only procedural matters. A new disappointment for the family: the court declared that the statute of limitations on the action had passed;

the Wildensteins should have brought their suit within three months of the publication of Feliciano's book *The Lost Museum*.

This troubling story, on which I shall not attempt to give an opinion beyond citing the three successive rulings of the French judicial system, casts a deep shadow over my grandmother's love affair.

Did their relationship last for a long time? At this point it would be virtually impossible to tell. But who, really, was this man who slipped into my grandparents' lives, coming between them? Was he a passing fancy or an archrival delighted to destabilize his competitor? Could he have been worth the suffering he caused?

And who, really, was my grandmother? A passionate woman in need of love or a socialite fascinated by appearances? My grandfather was a good husband, in the sense of the phrase in those days, but in all likelihood he wasn't terribly exciting from a romantic point of view. My grandmother wanted to enjoy the carefree years between the wars. She was undoubtedly more hedonistic, more intoxicated by glamour than her husband, who was so preoccupied with the development of modern art. She wanted to dance, to enjoy herself, to be loved. He wanted only to work. This was the classic story of the romantic Emma and her stodgy Charles in *Madame Bovary*, or the flamboyant Ariane and the fool Adrien Deume in Albert Cohen's novel *Belle du Seigneur*. But my grandfather was neither a killjoy nor a petty bureaucrat; he was a curious and innovative spirit. All he needed to do was look away from his Picassos for a moment to gaze at the

Renoir—pretty, charming, and curvaceous—that he had in his bed.

Eighty years have passed since then. "Et la mer efface sur le sable / Les pas des amants désunis," as Jacques Prévert wrote and Yves Montand sang: "The sea washes away / The footprints of parted lovers in the sand."

PI-AR-ENCO

New York, once my family's city of refuge, and also my birthplace. The family archives are still on East Seventy-ninth Street, in the four-story town house that was home to the last Galerie Rosenberg.

My grandfather, who arrived with his wife and daughter in the autumn of 1940, initially moved into a house closer to midtown, on East Fifty-seventh Street, where he set up his gallery in 1941 and which he left thirteen years later.

I have few memories of Fifty-seventh Street. Paul rented that stately old house, owned by the queen of England, who had a considerable property portfolio in Manhattan, but he had grown weary of the old building and wanted to live in a home of his own.

He bought his house on Seventy-ninth Street, between Madison and Fifth avenues, from Chester Dale, one of his major clients. After a lot of renovation, the family moved into the building in 1953. Paul was seventy-one. He lived there for only six years, increasingly passing responsibility for the running of the gallery to my uncle Alexandre.

This location on the prosperous Upper East Side, a bit sedate but elegant, wasn't a bad spot for business in the 1950s. In setting up shop there, my grandfather started a trend among gallery owners. Soon all his competitors who had established their galleries in midtown, just as he had, moved north, to within a few blocks of his new address at 20 East Seventy-ninth Street. By the time I was a child, it was bustling with art dealers.

—

Paul Rosenberg and Company was the name of the business. PR & Co. "Pi-ar-enco" to my childish ears, making me wonder what crazy-sounding person we were sharing our house with. I spent so many childhood Christmases there that until recently New York was an enchanted place as far as I was concerned.

My parents and I had returned to France when I was three, but I loved that town house on Seventy-ninth Street, every corner of which I knew so well. It was a beautiful limestone building, typical of New York, opulent looking, and right beside Central Park. In fact, it was just a few steps away from one of just two roads that ran all the way through to the west side of the park. I loved the sound of the crosstown bus that stopped before the front door. It was for me the sound of New York. Yes, New York was magical. With smoke billowing out of the street, it seemed the opposite of Paris, where I was living in a very quiet street near the Bois de Boulogne, in the Sixteenth Arrondissement. Today the building belongs to my aunt Elaine, Alexandre's widow, my mother's brother having died in 1987 at the age of sixty-six.

—

The steps were once framed by Rodin's *Thinker* and its companion, *The Age of Bronze.* But the black-and-white marble mosaics of the entrance hall—similar to those in rue La Boétie—are still there, as they were in the exhibition halls that I wasn't allowed to enter as a small child. The elevator, modern in the 1950s, is practically an antique today, with its sliding aluminum door. I know by heart the sound it makes and the way it slows, shuddering, as it reaches each floor. My parents and I lived on the third floor, but I sometimes slipped out on the floor below, hoping to spot some "clients," as my grandfather grandly called them, although I couldn't see how they were any more important than the customers at the Zitomer pharmacy on the corner of Seventy-eighth Street and Madison.

My grandparents shared a bedroom in their apartment on the second floor but had separate bathrooms, which always intrigued me. The television was in their bedroom, and it was there that I saw my first westerns, vintage ones with cowboys and Indians, covered wagons in a circle, and flaming arrows. The first television shows too, with women in New Look fashions created by Christian Dior in the fifties: women in wide gathered skirts and crewneck twinsets. There weren't many anchorwomen, no women journalists; women just presented the commercials—so deliciously dated today—for huge blue and pink American cars that created Detroit and then left it in ruins, cars you come across only in Cuba these days: "See the USA in your Chevrolet" . . . The refrain from the 1950s still echoes in my head.

—

New York was snow, Central Park, my sled, and the magic of the Santas ringing their bells to draw in the window-shoppers outside Bloomingdale's.

New York was chocolate sundaes spilling over with whipped cream in the modern ice-cream parlors with their fake red leather banquettes, my first Walt Disney cartoons, mountains of toys at FAO Schwarz, on the corner of Fifth Avenue and East Fifty-eighth Street where the iciest gusts in the city blew, but where children like me were warmed by the consoling sight of those immense teddy bears that we never bought but that filled our dreams.

Above all, New York meant a month off from school, the only drawback being the math lessons my mother insisted on giving me. Faced with my inability to grasp problems about the distances between train tracks and the gaps between fence posts, she would end up throwing pencils and scraps of paper at me, telling me I'd never make anything of myself. The pencils were the ones with which Americans wrote on lined yellow paper—the "legal pads" you see in *Mad Men*—less formal than the shiny sheets in my Parisian Clairefontaine school notebooks.

Fifty years later on TV, I see Obama's advisers coming out of the West Wing carrying the same lined yellow pads and those inevitable sharpened pencils, blissfully unaware that those same pencils once grazed the head of a little math dunce. This is the retro side of an America that still prefers its shops to have old wooden doors with rattling, gilded knobs rather than the big glass doors that open automatically as soon as you cross the threshold of any French pharmacy.

New York meant endless family discussions between parents and grandparents about France, which was imploding, even though news of the unstable Fourth Republic* reached us only in fragments. Politics? It was talked about, of course. As a little girl I vaguely understood that it was a world intended for grown-ups, something grave and mysterious, to which I was unbelievably lucky to have been exposed.

I had always preferred to act beyond my years around things I didn't understand. Before I was even two years old, I imitated my parents by pretending to read *The New York Times*—if upside down. At four, I assumed a look of great concentration when my father summoned me to discuss what he called serious matters. This happened whenever governments fell, every month or so. My father would address me, struggling not to laugh: "Anne, some serious things are happening: the cabinet [that was

---

*The regime that was in effect from the end of World War II through its collapse in 1958, when de Gaulle established the Fifth Republic.

what the government was called in those days] has been overturned."

"Oh!" I would say, horrified at the apocalyptic vision he had just evoked, because the word for "cabinet" also meant "water closet." "Something has to be done." My father went on. "Me, I'll take charge of foreign affairs." "Me, I'll take the train," I invariably replied, without understanding a word he was saying, but delighted that my beloved father thought me a worthy partner for his grown-up conversations. My grandfather would burst out laughing, and I was very proud to amuse my family even without understanding what was so funny. On reflection, I took my first steps in political debate at the town house on Seventy-ninth Street, an experience that must have stayed with me in my twenty years as a political journalist in France.

New York in those days was synonymous with happiness, treats, holidays. My parents and I went there at first by ocean liner, which meant four or five long seasick days, and then, before the first Boeing flights began, by Super Constellations, big carrier planes that stopped at Shannon in Ireland and at Gander in the northeast of Newfoundland.

Pinned to my little coat was the Cours Hattemer, the "cross of honor," awarded by my school to the term's best pupils. It was utterly ridiculous, that cross, a miniature copy of the Croix de la Légion d'Honneur. On the bus, passengers would ask my mother what heroic deeds I had performed to deserve that military-style decoration.

—

As New York winters were notoriously harsh, my grandfather's frail condition meant that he didn't go out much. His health had further deteriorated over the previous few years after a stroke that, while leaving his mind intact, deprived him of fluent speech and gave him a dreadful stammer. I was sometimes frightened by his damaged voice and by his little finger, gnarled with arthritis.

—

In Paris, Paul and I often visited his colleagues, outings that I found slightly boring, but that were always followed by a fresh-squeezed orange juice at the Relais du Bois in the Bois de Boulogne, where we drank in silence to keep from frightening the squirrels.

One day he took me to see Paul Pétridès, who ran a well-known gallery but whose reputation had been tarnished by collaborationist activities during the war. Back in the car, Paul grumbled, "That man is a pheasant," which seemed an odd expression to use for someone. When I asked what he meant, he said he was referring to a rotten game bird. I brought that hunting term back home with me, much to my family's amusement.

My grandfather had an amazing eye: long after looking at a painting that he found interesting at a colleague's gallery, he would ruminate over it. Driving toward the Bois de Boulogne, he would suddenly announce: "That painting is a fake!"

—

Every summer, I set off with my grandparents for the south of France, along the old Route Nationale 7, a road lined with plane trees that were magnificent to look at but lethally distracting to those driving cars. The highway leading to the south didn't yet exist, and it took us three full days to get to Cannes. We always stopped at the same places—Saint-Étienne on the first day, Avignon and Aix on the second day—before we arrived, the third stop being on the shores of the Mediterranean. Once we were there, within two days we absolutely had to go to the Galerie Maeght in Saint Paul de Vence and above all to see Picasso in Mougins.

By visiting museums with my grandfather—the Louvre, one bit at a time, the Orangerie, and the Musée d'Art Moderne—I learned what was worth looking at and what wasn't worth so much as a second glance. The quality of the works was gauged by the speed with which I crossed those exhibition halls at my grandfather's side. The Flemish masters or, of course, the Italian quattrocento were carefully examined, but paintings of the French and English seventeenth and eighteenth centuries were skipped over. The Gainsboroughs, with their very English solemnity, weren't considered particularly noteworthy. Our interest revived again with Corot (at last), Courbet, and, obviously, the impressionists. Looking at certain paintings by fashionable painters—I'm thinking of Bernard Buffet, for example, whom Paul couldn't stand—Paul allowed himself the luxury of saying that "they weren't worth a fig." Some were simply declared "ugly" or "without genius," if not "without talent." Various minor paintings by Renoir, Gauguin, or Monet were decreed "too red" or "too dark," "too vague" or "too soft," "lacking mastery" or "lacking power." And these judgments, fifty years on, still have the force of law as far as I'm concerned. "Don't waste your eyes," my grandfather would say to me, "on works that are not exceptional." The moderns—Braque, Matisse, Léger, and, above all, Picasso: they were his world.

But that gentle life belonged to Paris. In New York the rhythm was different: my grandfather worked, I strolled about the city with my mother and my grandmother, and for the child I was in those days it was a paradise.

—

During the winter of 2009 I couldn't wait to board the train from where I was living in Washington, D.C., to get back to New York, to East Seventy-ninth Street. That's where the gallery's archives are kept, devotedly guarded by my aunt Elaine, who worshipped her father-in-law. She had done a marvelous job organizing all this material with the help of an archivist from the Museum of Modern Art, to which the papers had been donated.

I immersed myself in those files for days at a time, in the course of several visits. An old desk in a little room, six feet by ten, windowless—I'm sure it's the room where I suffered my mathematical torments—but with a skylight, rather gloomy, old linoleum, all on the same floor where I had lived with my parents as a child.

The internal staircase that leads both to this room and to my aunt's apartment is the one on which I used to hide. Often when I couldn't sleep, I would sit on the steps, hiding in a corner, and try to make out what the grown-ups were saying downstairs. From there, I would also listen to the classical music that my uncle was passionate about. And so it was, that in my pajamas I was allowed to listen to my first concerts of baroque music. I remember noticing, for example, that Georges Bizet had borrowed his tune for *L'Arlésienne* from a theme by Michel-Richard Delalande, and having heard my grandmother humming the music from *Carmen* when I was very young, I felt it was a dreadful fraud.

—

My aunt wonders about my recent obsession with a grandfather and a family history that I'd barely acknowledged until now. She and my mother didn't really get on and never truly understood each other. My mother was so close to her brother that my aunt often felt excluded. Alexandre seemed to pay my mother more attention than he did his wife. Not surprisingly, this caused my aunt, who was excluded from the affairs of Pi-ar-enco on which my uncle faithfully reported to my mother, a great deal of torment.

In short, my aunt Elaine, still laser sharp and quick

on her feet at eighty-nine,* looks over my shoulder at the documents I'm consulting and the notes I take. Should I tell her that I'm feeling my way around the archive? She's taken the trouble to file away even the most insignificant scraps of paper from the Galerie Rosenberg. Should I express my surprise at my grandparents' personal life, which I'm sensing was more turbulent than legend allowed? I'm not sure. So I go on investigating, making sense of the voluminous papers as best I can.

Photographs of every prewar exhibition at rue La Boétie. Invoices for wine bought in 1928. Letters to Alfred Barr in the years before and after the war. Pieces of paper scribbled on by my grandfather, the beginning of an autobiography that wouldn't get beyond page ten. Fairly dry letters from Paul to unknown painters who wanted him to represent them. A bill from a picture framer in the 1920s and, most of all, telegrams or letters from 1942 revealing the ignorance of refugees about what was happening in occupied France. Files in Russian too, containing archives looted from the gallery in Paris by the Germans in 1940, then by the Russians in Berlin in 1945, carefully filed away in big boxes with titles written in Cyrillic. These archives were recovered a few years ago, thanks entirely to the perseverance of my cousin Elisabeth and the postglasnost transparency of the Russian authorities, who gave them to the French government, which in turn was gracious enough to restore them to us.

---

*Ninety-three, in 2014.

That precious immersion in the family archives on Seventy-ninth Street allowed me to reconstruct my grandfather's life after the upheavals of the 1940s. Upheavals, sure. But at the same time, he felt close to this continent, which he had so loved exploring twenty years before.

A LONG RELATIONSHIP

Paul knew America quite well, as he had tried hard to establish his beloved modern painters across the Atlantic.

John Quinn, an American lawyer and collector, corresponded with Paul in the 1920s and tried to explain to him that his efforts to sell modern art in America were premature. "Just five or six years ago," he explains in a letter found in the family archives, "Knoedler had put on a Cézanne exhibition and people laughed, which they wouldn't do now . . ." In May 1922, Quinn tried to convince Paul that no New York gallery, "not Knoedler, Gimpel, Wildenstein or Durand-Ruel, will show any Picassos because their clients aren't open to this kind of painting. Dealers don't believe in modern art."

But Paul persisted. He was in Chicago that same year. And from New York to Kansas City, of all places, he preached contemporary art and was keen, in spite of the lack of enthusiasm from the American public, to show his beloved Matisse, Picasso, and Braque to the New World, which didn't get it at all.

On November 23, 1923, Paul put on—probably at the Georges Wildenstein Gallery, with which he was affiliated at the time in the transatlantic representation of Picasso's works—the Spanish painter's first New York show. He wrote to Picasso, "Your exhibition is a great success, and like all great successes, we're not selling a thing! You'd have to be mad like me, or a crank like me, to embark on such an undertaking."

In a letter written to Picasso in November 1923, he was critical of America: "Order reigns here, but there is a lack of European sophistication. The golden calf is more revered than ever, and the moneyed class is all that matters. Everything is colossal, even the museums. The worst of our painters is the best here . . . They have a collection of Rembrandts, just as I have a collection of Picassos, an incalculable number of them. Every self-respecting gallery has its Rembrandt or its Titian . . . Your paintings have arrived, they're wonderful, but I fear they don't like that kind of thing here. I'm expecting a vast crowd, meaning three visitors a day! . . . When nostalgia takes hold of me, I talk to my paintings, including yours. Ah, *mon cher Paris*, it's the only place one can live."

A few weeks later he looks more favorably on the excitement of New York: "I'm enjoying myself more: there's a spirit of will and strength," but he still rails against the aesthetic limitations of the Americans: "Your exhibition is a great succès d'estime. But while in Paris there would have been a great crush, not many people came. Out of a population of six million, sixty visitors a day! But it's all over the papers, so what do buyers need?

The New Continent doesn't go and see the New Painting, that is, the painting that is essentially timeless. They feel more at home with the painting of the past, with conventions."

In 1934, during one of his trips to New York, he writes to Picasso again. And he is still skeptical: "The Bonnard exhibition was totally unsuccessful here. It's too fine for them. Too tasteful. Too tasteful and without enough forms!"

Even at the start of the war, when he was still able to correspond with Matisse, he could be severe in his judgment of those citizens of the New World, after seeing portraits by Matisse and other French artists in *Life* magazine. "Very late," he notes, "because the ones shown have been established in the rest of the world for over thirty years! Better late . . ."[1]

—

In 1934 Paul decided to mount a major exhibition devoted to three great artists, Braque, Matisse, and Picasso. He wrote to Picasso: "This exhibition will do a lot of good because it brings to the eyes of the public the new forms of expression of artists they had heard about but never seen. The public is divided, they all stay for a long time, upset that they don't understand . . . My previous exhibition, from Ingres to Cézanne, was splendid, but its splendor was rehashed. It was from the past, and there was no merit in admiring works that, dating as they did from 1814 to 1910, have had time to enter men's minds. But this exhibition represents our era, more than thirty-three years of our lives. Since it is the first of this kind, it has an absolute virginity, it must create the same effect as the impressionist show."

He himself attended to the smallest details of the exhibition, just as he did in Paris, and sent Picasso the plans for the hanging of each individual painting. "Evidence of the power [of your paintings]. I had to balance them out with two Braques!" These words, which might come across as so much flummery, are in fact meant quite sincerely. Paul was not given to effusive language. He could even be severe in his judgment of certain contemporary geniuses who were recognized as such, not least by him. "The only weak point is Matisse," Paul writes. "He can't take it. He flickers and goes out between the two of you [Braque and Picasso]. He . . . has forgotten about forms and volumes. Color is too important and you have the feeling you could add layers of color by painting the walls themselves. And that gives a sense of painted canvases, while you are creating the sense of colored sculptures." To me this assessment seems unfair because the light that floods Matisse's paintings makes them masterpieces in blue or yellow. It's true that Matisse's work, which is more accessible than that of the great abstractionists, struck Paul as more decorative and less innovative.

In that same letter Paul spoke bitterly about a different exhibition elsewhere in the city—apparently dedicated to artists he didn't represent—that enjoyed great success with the public, "with 2,000 idiotic paintings that represented the most grotesque parodies imaginable. People must actually realize this! But I shall stick my neck out and say that stupidity and bad faith will always pre-vail among the living, and both of us may be in our graves when the same people's descendants glorify this art, de-molishing the achievements of the creative generations to which you yourselves have given birth . . . But Galileo is right, 'eppur si muove' nothing will stop the progress of truth; beauty will always be beauty."

Sadly, this country, which my grandfather had ini-tially seen as a continent to explore, was about to become his land of exile.

THE WAR YEARS
IN NEW YORK

Paul disembarked in New York with his wife and daughter in September 1940. They stayed at the Hotel Madison on Fifty-eighth Street until Paul decided to rent a new gallery on Fifty-seventh Street in 1941. Still in the throes of despair, Paul remained as anxious as refugees throughout the ages have been: "No one can understand how comforted I felt when an immigration officer said to me, 'Don't worry, you're among friends now.'"

He managed to correspond with France to a certain extent. His letters seemed to reach Nice, at any rate, in the unoccupied zone, where Matisse was still living. On November 27, 1940, he writes to the painter from his hotel room: "I don't yet know what I'm going to do, but I might settle here as I did in Paris . . . No news of Pablo, or the other Parisians, which disturbs and worries me. I have in front of me a Cézanne of the area around Aix, with an atmosphere so clear and pure that it delights my eyes and sings to my heart."

Grieving for his gallery on rue La Boétie, Paul corresponds with his painter friend as frequently as possible: "We miss your paintings here because we've severed contact with Europe. The market needs your works, the American school is already taking advantage of this. They're bringing out all the Sunday painters, people who started painting when they were 72 and who are 92 now. I'm going to San Francisco to give a lecture as I did in Chicago, about art in general and about all of you in particular. It's the only thing that amuses or interests me. Too many things that I was once fond of, which were my life, are far away from me now. Even the beautiful countryside of Provence, that mild, gentle light, that serene landscape, comes to mind as I write to you." He continues, on February 18, 1941, after Matisse has had surgery and Paul is inquiring after his health: "You are lucky to have painting; by creating you forget the hardships and anxiety of our times. Separation is painful, because everything I love is far from me." He adds in semicoded language, alluding to the last canvases that he had bought from the artist and that he suspected had been stolen from him: "I don't know what became of your children of 1940. They were close to my heart, they were my joy. What can we do to get them back . . . [?]"[1]

In November and December 1940, in two letters to his son Pierre, who had himself opened a gallery in New York, Matisse asks for news of his dealer and friend, disguising his name for the benefit of the censor who opened the mail: "How is Paul Floirac? Tell him plenty of things from me, but don't tell him that I'm writing to tell you that Pablo is worried about his future. Essentially he has lots of resources, and might return to his Blue or Rose periods, which are still highly prized."[2]

Paul becomes increasingly homesick and loses contact with his family, who remained in Paris and miraculously escaped the roundups of the Jewish population, as well as his friends. Though he is anxious about the situation in occupied France, he's unable to find out much.

Later, in March 1942, he writes to his friend Henri de Vilmorin: "You must have news about France and know what's happening there. The massacre of innocent people, whether from malnutrition or from cold, whether from diseases contracted in the concentration camps . . . Oh, how our brothers are suffering, and I imagine their pain at seeing our beautiful country looted and exploited by its enemies . . . Luckily we are confident and we have the firm hope that we will once again see the whole country purged and regenerated."

Paul is frustrated, going on about feelings of impotence in the face of war, and tries to make himself useful. His wife and especially his daughter are working for France Forever. He himself organizes benefit exhibitions for the Free French, donating considerable sums to the effort. In February 1941 Paul gives the Free French Relief Committee a Stinson 105, the first air ambulance to be deployed in French Equatorial Africa. General Edgard de Larminat, one of the first French officers to have joined the Free French Forces, who is later made a Compagnon de la Libération, sends a telegram of appreciation from Brazzaville to the "generous donor" who wishes to remain anonymous.

Paul, in a state of agitation, writes to absolutely everyone. To his French friends, even though there is no hope that his letters will reach them. To his comrade and modern art collector Alphonse Kann, who is in England. To the efficient and generous secretary in his London office, Winifred Easton, who is taking care of the "children" that arrived in June 1940 and who is to survive the blitz: "I know you are working hard, and that your morale has not been affected. We too are keeping our chins up, and we do not doubt for a second that we have been through the worst of the war, and that the end will soon come, with victory for all of us. Yes, the situation in France is terrible. That is why we are working so hard to identify and describe those horrendous characters who are insulting the reality of my country. We are publishing pamphlets and books that show the true face of France. But don't worry: when the war is over, the French will sweep all that aside, and those who did not resist will perhaps pay with their lives for the dirty job they've done . . ." This letter, with its forced optimism, dates from October 1942, the darkest hours of Europe at war.

—

Paul is consumed with worry about Alexandre, having had no news of him since he left England, except that he is somewhere in Africa. Naively, he imagines that he might be granted leave. He doesn't know that this is the eve of the Normandy landings. On May 24, 1944, he writes to Guérin de Beaumont, the agent general for the Provisional Government of the French Republic in New

York, hoping in vain to have Kiki brought over, after having been separated from him since June 1940: "We're very depressed. His mother is in despair. It's really a miracle that she goes on despite her enormous pain . . . As for my own personal activities, apart from the Renoir Centenary exhibition organized for the benefit of the Free French Relief Committee, and the exhibition of Cézanne's works organized for France Forever and the Fighting French Committee, I don't need to mention them. My every action is that of a patriot who loves his country, particularly when it is in danger. I can say that I have spent my whole life fighting against the Germans who are after me, and that if I had stayed in France I would certainly have been taken hostage and faced the firing squad a long time ago."

In fact, he will find out nothing for a long time, either about the atrocities of the Nazis and their Vichy accomplices or about the looting. Above all, this "patriot," as he terms himself, is unaware that on July 23, 1940, while he was still in Portugal, a law stripping nationality of any French citizen who has gone abroad was passed by Vichy France.

Though he probably did know that on October 3, *Le Journal officiel* published the Jewish Statute, with its notorious Article 1: "In terms of the application of the present law, any person will be regarded as Jewish if he is descended from three grandparents of the Jewish race or two grandparents of the same race if the spouse is also a Jew." After this come prohibitions concerning posts or honors awarded by the state and access to teaching positions, the army, high administration, or the courts. Jews would also be excluded from journalism and the management of newspapers, as well as work in cinema or the theater.

The Casino de Paris, other clubs, and certain parks and gardens were "forbidden to dogs and Jews," as the signs put it. But as the writer Dan Franck notes bitterly, "the duck with blood sauce at the Tour d'Argent retained its reputation."[3] Franck also relates how the Opéra and its director, Serge Lifar, a French ballet dancer and choreographer, welcomed Hitler and Goebbels, and how the young Herbert von Karajan conducted *Tristan and Isolde* there. As for the famous actor Sacha Guitry, "all was just fine."

Paul knew only scraps of all this. One thing he was certainly in the dark about was the deportations that followed upon the loss of nationality. On February 23, 1942, an order decreed the "denationalization" of Paul Rosenberg and his family. These orders complemented the law of July 23, 1940.

A month later, on March 26, 1942, Paul sent a telegram to "The President of the Commission for the Examination of Cases of Forfeiture of Nationality, Ministry of Justice, Vichy, France," stating: "I am learning of my denationalization by order of 23 February 1942. Protest energetically and have strong reservations. Letter follows." A letter, addressed to the same commission, did in fact follow, on April 16, 1942, revealing great ignorance of the situation as well as total candor. Five pages in which Paul made rather clumsy attempts at self-justification: "I learn that by an order of 23 February 1942, in accordance with the law of 23 July 1940, I have been stripped of French nationality for leaving France without a valid reason, between 10 May and 30 June 1940 . . . I protest indignantly against the interpretation of the aforementioned text as regards my case . . . I have always fulfilled all my duties, my past is one of honor and probity, etc." This is a "flagrant injustice . . . It was only during my stay in Portugal that I discovered the conditions of the armistice. This prompted me to continue my journey. In fact, after some reflection, I determined that I could make myself more useful by staying in the United States than by going back to France . . . Being stripped of one's nationality implies a dishonor that no worthy man can accept without attempting to defend himself. I am not begging for clemency for a crime I have not committed, but calling for justice to which I have a right like any other citizen."

The opening words of this letter reflect the state of mind of French Jews in 1940: unable to believe that while they were good enough to serve as cannon fodder in the First World War, they could be dismissed as traitors twenty years later just because they had been born Jewish. We come across this uncomprehending reaction in every country that has known discrimination and deportations, even in the state of mind of the people crammed into the cattle cars. It was impossible for a sane mind to imagine the Shoah in 1940.

Paul obviously knew little about what was happening in his homeland. He had asked his friend Gilbert Lévy, in whom he had complete trust, to keep his papers and to ensure that wages were paid to the staff who remained at the gallery. To Lévy, who was to be deported and gassed in Auschwitz while one of his sons fought with my uncle Alexandre in the African campaign and died in his arms in Normandy, he writes with disconcerting naiveté on March 20, 1942: "I learn that I've been denationalized. Can you contact my brother, as I am asking him to find a lawyer should I need to defend my case to the commission[?]" Paul was as yet unaware that there are some cases that cannot be pleaded.

—

But let's return to the letter my scandalized grandfather sent to Vichy in 1942. The last paragraph, about the dishonor inflicted and the refusal to ask for a pardon that he judged to be defamatory, captures his state of mind. On the other hand, the feeble excuse that he would be more useful to France in the United States does not seem to match his indignation. My grandparents fled because their lives were in jeopardy, and they had no need to be ashamed. Yet admitting that others stayed on in their homeland and actually risked and often paid with their lives undoubtedly filled him with shame.

As Emmanuelle Loyer writes, "Unlike the history of Poland, in which the exile is integral to the national story of the last two centuries, the French tradition is characterized by a disparaging image of the exile, which places him somewhere between flight and treason . . . Since the French Revolution, the exile has been accused of anti-patriotism, and assimilation is seen as an active metonymy of the France of the Counterrevolution."[4]

Paul experienced the loss of his nationality inflicted by a regime he loathed as a wound and humiliation that imposed upon him a constant need for self-justification. If he had no plans to move his gallery back to Paris after the war and chose instead to stay in New York, it was probably because the art market was more vigorous there, although many Parisian art dealers, beginning with Kahn-weiler, did prosper in France after the liberation. But the deepest reason was that unlike the French, who had stripped him of his nationality and some of whom were even involved in the theft of his property and would doubtless have had him deported, the Americans welcomed him along with his family, protected him, and enabled him to relaunch his career. They recognized him as a great practitioner of his trade and helped him recover his soiled dignity.

I found the same tone in my father's war diary. Demobilized in 1940, unable to bear life in occupied France, he managed to leave for the United States. Once in New York, he felt very uneasy about being "sheltered." He enrolled as a noncommissioned officer with the Free French and embarked with two compatriots on a British troop carrier, the only Frenchmen among eight thousand American soldiers. Traveling via South America and the Cape of Good Hope, he eventually came back up the Red Sea, disembarked, and went on fighting.

My father kept a journal throughout those three years, and even in his account of that two-month zigzag voyage across an ocean infested with mines and German submarines, followed by his time fighting for the Free French

Forces in Beirut and Cairo, he expresses a constant need to rehabilitate himself, to "redeem" himself for his supposed passivity. Consumed with anxiety about his relatives who had stayed in Paris or were hidden away somewhere in France, he was hardly any happier about his life as a Gaullist envoy to the Middle East than he was with his life as a refugee in New York.

My grandfather would refuse all contact with Vichy to "plead his own case." To someone who had suggested acting as an intermediary, he wrote on April 24, 1942: "Given recent events in France, I do not wish to communicate in any way with a government run by a man like Laval.* I would rather lose all I possess."

And that was what happened to his paintings, indeed to his illusions of a just world.

---

*Pierre Laval (1883–1945) served as prime minister of France from 1931 to 1932, as vice president of Vichy's Council of Ministers in 1940, and as head of government from 1942 to 1944. Convicted of high treason, he was executed in 1945.

PREOCCUPATIONS
OF THE HEART

My grandfather thought constantly about the lives of the painters who stayed behind in France, hoping they would be hostile to the occupying forces. Some of them were, but overall, the artists who remained in Paris didn't distinguish themselves one way or another. "As soon as the Nazis were the adversaries of culture and freedom, any free expression of the spirit became an act of courage," wrote Laurence Bertrand Dorléac.[1]

In fact, as Paul suspected, Braque, Matisse, and Picasso showed no sympathy for the Germans. Other artists, like André Derain, Otto Friesz, van Dongen, Paul Belmondo, and de Vlaminck, did not hesitate to go on tour in Germany. Some even returned as propagandists, so in thrall were they with the Nazi regime.

Braque wasn't even invited along. "Fortunately my painting didn't please them; I wasn't invited, otherwise, perhaps I would have gone, on account of the promised exchange of prisoners," he candidly confessed in retrospect.[2] He had been a close friend of Derain, who had taken this politically charged tour, but he had no wish to disavow him. As Braque's biographer Alex Danchev writes, "He was a *moraliste*, not a moralizer . . . But something was broken. Braque and Derain were never as close again."[3]

Paul was aware that Braque was no activist and that a painting like *Guernica* was not his style. Besides, Braque could not understand Picasso's commitment to communism or, later on, his decision to paint a peace dove. Braque's sole concern was the validity of his art. "There is no scream in Braque, just a whisper," Danchev explains.[4] But the war destabilized him, and he even dreamed of going to Switzerland. For the first time since 1917 he had stopped painting, as he wrote to my grandfather when Paul was still near Bordeaux, in Floirac.

After he returned to Paris and before settling in Pacy-sur-Eure, where his aged mother lived, Braque started painting very dark still lifes (including his famous black fish). Until 1943, only his two great writer friends Jean Paulhan and Francis Ponge, both *résistants*, had the privilege of seeing his paintings.

But in 1943, a small exhibition was held in a room dedicated to Braque in the Salon d'Automne and hailed by the collaborationist Pierre Drieu La Rochelle, but denounced by Lucien Rebatet in *Je suis partout*, the emblematic publication of the collaboration.

Georges Braque had rejected the advances of the Reich, refused to prostrate himself before the Reich's official sculptor, Arno Breker, unlike Jean Cocteau, and dared turn up at the funeral of Max Jacob, who had died to general indifference in Drancy, shortly before his convoy left for Auschwitz. Braque also declined Marshal Pétain's invitation to design the Vichy emblem, "Work, Family, Homeland." "He wasn't part of the Resistance. But he was dignified," writes Dan Franck, "a serious quality in a time of compromises."[5] My grandfather, who for his article in *Art in Australia* imagined Braque "in blue smock, confined to his home, standing before his easel, his pots of colour ground by himself, hand full of brushes, creating another new canvas for our pleasure," was right about the character of his old friend, to whom he displayed the most brotherly attachment. Paul described Braque as being very different from Picasso, "always placid and a quiet conversationalist."[6] "He never sings out of tune," Picasso once declared about him. "He seeks only harmonies and symphonies in his canvases. There is never the clash of colour like some strident note of a cymbal or trumpet. He represents all the beautiful French tradition of Corot, Chardin, and like these painters he is full of humility.

"Like Picasso," my grandfather continued, "he [Braque] never paints from nature. His works are re-creations . . . He is never a mixer, living quite isolated, abhorring honours and receptions . . . The sight of certain uniforms must trouble his heart and soul."[7]

Paul was severe in his judgment of artists like Derain when he learned that they had accepted Vichy honors, but he moderated his condemnation. In August 1942, according to papers found in the family archive, Paul abandoned an exhibition of twentieth-century artists in New

York: "It is impossible to show artists who have been in Germany, while at the same time it is not a French custom to condemn people without having heard their side of the story, so it is impossible to hold this exhibition."

He was mistaken about other standard-bearers for fauvism, such as de Vlaminck, however, believing that they were resisting the occupying forces. Conversely, de Vlaminck, who was jealous of Picasso, took advantage of the occupation to tear into "that Catalan with the look of a monk and the eyes of an inquisitor," as he wrote in the magazine *Comœdia*. "Cubism! Perversity of spirit, inadequacy, amoralism, as far from painting as pederasty is from love."[8]

Picasso couldn't afford to reply. He had left rue La Boétie, where the Nazis were now his next-door neighbors, and was living at 7 rue des Grands-Augustins, in an apartment found by Dora Maar, his companion at the time. He represented "the ultimate scapegoat meant to embody the thousand and one facets of evil, displacement, disorder and blasphemy," writes Dorléac.[9] The Gestapo could have arrested the painter at any time, but at Cocteau's request, he was given some protection on the German side by the all-powerful sculptor Arno Breker.

—

Since Picasso had opposed Franco very early on in the conflict, the republicans had appointed him honorary director in exile of the Prado. After the April 26, 1937, bombing of the small Basque village of Guernica on a market day by the German pilots of the Condor Legion,

Picasso, who had been commissioned to create a mural for the Spanish Republic Pavilion at the Universal Exhibition in Paris, painted *Guernica*, one of his greatest masterpieces. Picasso never forgot that Pétain had been the French ambassador to Franco's Spain, which may also explain his antipathy toward the Vichy regime.

There is a legend about this world-famous painting. German officers, visiting Picasso in his studio in rue des Grands-Augustins and seeing that most accusatory of paintings in a corner, were said to have asked him: "Did you do that?" According to legend, the painter shot back, "No, you did." A sublimely dramatic reply, although I suspect it may be apocryphal. My grandfather and my mother visited Picasso in the same studio just after the liberation. As they congratulated him on the courageous statements he had made, statements that had crossed the seas as a symbol of the resistance of artists and intellectuals to the occupying forces, Picasso replied, slightly embarrassed, "Yes, I must have said something like that. Well, all right, let's say I did . . ." This was a story often told by my grandfather and later by my mother.

But I have no other evidence of Paul and Picasso's discussing the war, not even at its start. At that point in early 1940, Picasso was at Royan, a small fishing village on the Atlantic coast, while my grandparents were living in Floirac. In any case, the letters don't so much as mention the declaration of war on September 3, 1939. Perhaps they spoke on the phone that day.

On October 25, 1939, Paul alludes to the war when he sends birthday wishes to "mon vieux Pic," roughly two months before his own: "It's a sad birthday," he writes. On December 29, 1939, Paul, who turned fifty-eight that day, sends Picasso "my best wishes for 1940. You will cost me two times two 30 franc stamps for the telegram. And yet our authorities said we had to economize!"

So the war always seems to be mentioned with some detachment in the correspondence between the future refugee and the Spanish republican. Certainly, this battle-free conflict must have seemed like an abstraction at that point, but I am still struck by the fact that there was so little room for it in their exchanges, in which they continue to "talk paintings." My grandmother even sent a message to Picasso expressing her relief that my grandfather finally had paintings on his walls in Floirac, which had been bare until then. He had in fact had them sent from Paris, thinking they would be safe south of the Loire. "Your paintings from 1940 are in the dining room," Paul writes. These were probably the tormented paintings the artist made that year, such as the *Standing Female Nude*, cited by Laurent Fabius as an example of the art of a painter devastated by the war.[10] "Thanks to you," Paul continues, "our meals are less monotonous, your canvases provoke both appreciation and hilarity."[11] In the same letter, he announces the death of Diola, his children's dog; my uncle Alexandre gave the dog's name to the plane he piloted in the Second Armored Division.

The last letter from Paul to Picasso, before they met again in the painter's studio on rue des Grands-Augustins, is dated May 9, 1940, the eve of the Nazis' offensive in which the Allies were taken by surprise in the Ardennes. Paul tells Picasso about his plan to go to Paris on May 14. After all, for almost everyone, this phase of the war—which became known as the Phoney War—had turned out to be only virtual. My grandfather fled Floirac through Spain and Portugal one month later.

—

And yet Picasso is very attuned to current events. During the Phoney War, he takes a quick trip to Paris from Royan. It's spring 1940, and Picasso bumps into Matisse. "Where are you going like that?" asks Picasso. "To see my tailor," replies Matisse. "What, you don't know that the front has been broken? The Germans will be in Paris by tomorrow!" "What about our generals?" Matisse asks him. Picasso looks at him seriously and replies (his response is in all the books): "*Our* generals are equivalent to the École des Beaux-Arts!" Which tells us a lot about both these painters' attitudes toward that school, so fearful of innovation, as well as of the French Army, which was stuck in the days of the First World War.

—

Picasso returned to the capital after the armistice. Why did he stay in Paris? My grandfather thought he was frightened by the idea of exile. "Staying wasn't a form of courage, but . . . of inertia," Picasso later said to Jean Leymarie, an art critic and the future director of the Musée d'Art Moderne.[12] Picasso wanted to devote himself exclusively to his work.

In 1943, Picasso met Françoise Gilot, who became his companion and the mother of two of his four children, Claude and Paloma. Around that time he invited to his house some of his politically committed friends, figures like poet Robert Desnos, but he didn't join the Resistance, as his friend Paul Éluard had done. "He refused the Germans' coal, and the material advantages they wanted to give him," writes Franck.[13] "He was primarily concerned about his artistic work. Picasso was entering an intensely prolific phase that was to last the rest of his life, and he abstained from anything that kept him away from that 'galleon's rhythm.' "[14]

In 1941 Paul imagined his Pic in a state of revolt, since he was "the freest of men." "What pleasure can he possibly have in painting now?" Paul wonders. "It had always been his joy to confront a canvas, mold it, work it meticulously in terms of depth, form and color, knead it, even torture it, and force it to give way to his titanic will."[15] That suffering doubtless existed, as did the artist's anxiety and discomfort with fascism. But they didn't stop him from making art.

In April 1940 Picasso had once more petitioned for naturalization, but this had been refused on the grounds of his alleged anarchist sympathies. He chose to stay, even though he still feared being handed over to Franco. Police reports from 1939—they would still have been the police of the Third Republic—had him on record for making "anti-French" statements at the Café de Flore. "A curious way of thanking the country that welcomed him, and in the current circumstances his conduct is inconvenient at the very least," said one police report of the time.

That same report, written even before the German invasion, stresses that "this foreigner who has made a reputation for himself in France in so-called modern art, allowing him to make considerable sums of money, is said to have declared several years ago to some of his friends that when he dies he wants to leave his collection to the Russian government and not to the French government." The stage was set for blacklists and xenophobia.

So Picasso was the holder of a residence permit, weirdly confused at the time with a kind of identity card, renewed on November 30, 1942, and valid until November 30, 1945. In the margin of the document was a note: "Catholic." And this, written by hand: "I certify on my honor that I am not Jewish in terms of the law of 2 June 1941"—the law that repeated and hardened the terms of the 1940 Jewish Statute. It was signed "Picasso."[16]

Troubling. Paul would have been shocked. But the artist needed to survive both the tragic events around him and the looting.

THE TRAIN, SCHENKER, AND THE ART OF THE POSSIBLE

August 27, 1944, and the troops of the Second Armored Division under the command of General Leclerc had just liberated Paris. Members of the Resistance had alerted them that a train containing one final convoy of looted works of art was about to leave the capital for Germany. A detachment of six volunteers, led by Lt. Alexandre Rosenberg, planned to stop the train at Aulnay, in the suburbs of Paris. On board were some dazed, homeward-bound old German soldiers and 148 crates of modern art, a small percentage of which belonged to the father of the lieutenant in question. Alexandre had last seen their contents on his parents' walls at 21 rue La Boétie, in 1939.

That train, which was leaving for Germany, was the final act of the huge program of looting that the Nazis had pursued in France and in all the countries of occupied Europe. Two weeks after the armistice, Hitler, on the pretext of bringing these works to safety, issued an order that all art objects belonging to the Jews should be "protected." "It is not an appropriation," said the memo that had come from Berlin, with the cynicism of those who think that the bigger the lie, the more likely it is to be believed, "but a transfer under our guard, as a guarantee for the peace negotiations."[1]

The first of the raids had begun in the summer of 1940. It was then, as the art historian and *résistant* Rose Valland writes, that "the German Embassy became the Nazi ministry of culture in an occupied country."[2] It was not until October 30, 1940, that about 450 crates left the rue de Lille (where the Reich Embassy was located) for the Musée du Jeu de Paume, to be submitted to the meticulous and systematic classification process perfected by the Einsatzstab Reichsleiter Rosenberg (ERR).

On July 4, 1940, Otto Abetz, the Reich ambassador in Paris, sent the Gestapo a list of the leading Jewish collectors and dealers in the city: Rothschild, Rosenberg, Bernheim-Jeune, Seligmann, Alphonse Kann, etc. It was on that day that the house at 21 rue La Boétie was sequestrated, along with the works of art that Paul had left there, a library of over twelve hundred books, all the furnishings (from the antique furniture to the kitchen utensils), several hundred photographic prints, and the whole of the gallery archives dating back to 1906.

The objects looted included a number of sculptures, which had remained in Paris because they were difficult to transport, among them a large Aristide Maillol and the two famous Auguste Rodin statues *Eve* and *The Bronze Age*, which had adorned the foyer. The same fate awaited *The Thinker*, which was recovered after the war and which as a child I saw so many times, welcoming visitors, while I looked down from the top of the stairs to the gallery at Seventy-ninth Street.

The French police supplied the trucks; the Gestapo, the men. As for the paintings that came from the most important collections in Paris, these were stacked up at the German Embassy.

The route taken by the stolen art objects is now well documented: the German forces looted about thirty-eight thousand apartments. The German dealer Gustav Rochlitz acted as a clearinghouse, exchanging the art favored by the Nazis—old masters—for works that appealed to Parisian dealers with their more contemporary taste. From this immense act of larceny perpetrated in France by the Nazis, about two thousand works have been recovered and remain unrestored to their rightful owners. Stamped "MNR," they belonged to families who had fled or been deported and will never return to claim them.

Including the paintings remaining at rue La Boétie, the 75 on the walls of the house in Floirac or rolled up in the garage there, and the 162 from the vault in Libourne, a total of 400 paintings were stolen from Paul. About 60 of them are still missing (are they in France, in Germany, in Russia?), most of which will probably never be found. The paintings that were recovered by Paul himself formed the inventory of the Seventy-ninth Street gallery, which has been almost entirely depleted since his death more than half a century ago.

Some of these works still show up from time to time, in estate sales or auctions. How I wish I could make them speak, so that they could tell the story of their odysseys, or rather of how they ended up tucked away in the apartments of families that never mentioned a word to anybody after fraudulently getting hold of them. In most cases the people who inherit them today know nothing of their provenance, which is buried along with the memory of those who appropriated them during those dark years.

—

After the conclusion of the last restitution cases in the mid-1960s, the subject of the looting of artworks during the Second World War remained hidden until the early 1990s, when the issue of the wartime persecution of the Jews in France slowly reemerged in the public eye. The books of Lynn Nicholas and Hector Feliciano also helped bring the issue back into public scrutiny.

In 1997 the Matteoli Commission, set up by Alain Juppé's government and continued under Lionel Jospin, was charged with studying the spoliation of Jewish assets during the occupation. "The looting had nothing to do with the circumstances born of the conditions of the victory of the Reich, but only with a fundamental and founding intention, matured and developed along with Nazi expansionism," as one of the contributors to the commission put it.[3]

In an article based on this investigation titled "From Spoliation to Restitution," Annette Wieviorka brings out the subtle distinction between spoliation and looting: "Spoliation, as defined by Gérard Lyon-Caen, is 'legal theft.' It is essentially a product of the Aryanization process, in which a property passes from 'Jewish' to 'Aryan' hands . . . Beyond the spoliation is the problem of looting. This is essentially undertaken by the German authorities. Two kinds are identified: First is targeted looting planned by the Germans. The Germans kept their eyes on the artworks of the great Jewish art dealers or collectors such as Alphonse Kann, Paul Rosenberg, Wildenstein, and the Rothschilds. This spectacular haul involved valuable works that were taken to Germany. The second type of looting began in 1942 and involved emptying Jewish apartments of all they contained."[4]

—

In the course of my research into the recovery of artworks owned by my grandfather, I discovered an extensive document that I'd never heard of before, the name of which reminded me of the title of the Steven Spielberg film *Schindler's List*. In contrast with the plot of that film about a righteous gentile who saved Jews from the Nazis, this is a collection of documents titled the Schenker Papers, which was declassified in 1995. Drawn up by the German Schenker transport company and reproduced on microfilm by the OSS, it lists the galleries and individuals that sold works of art to German museums, providing thirty-seven names. These include the dealers "who never declared sales made to the Germans, even though they had, to our knowledge, concluded numerous deals with the occupying forces—we have proof of it."[5] Among the names on this document were Martin Fabiani and Roger Dequoy, the latter being, as we have seen, employed by the

Wildenstein family, as manager of its gallery during the occupation.

An exhibition organized in 2008 by the Ministry of Culture, the Ministry of Foreign Affairs, the Direction des Musées de France, and the Réunion des Musées Nationaux, in collaboration with the Israel Museum in Jerusalem, set out a clear account of suspicious purchases made by equally suspicious dealers: "Martin Fabiani"—compromised in all the documents and quoted in the context of that exhibition—"sold many paintings during the Occupation and was found guilty for this after the liberation." My grandfather would describe Fabiani's reaction after being shown pictures of various paintings he was trying to retrieve. Fabiani denied having possessed any of them, including the ones he himself had returned to my grandfather. "He probably hadn't noticed," my grandfather said ironically, "that all the paintings stolen by the Germans bore on the back of the frame the words 'Paul Rosenberg—Bordeaux,' followed by the initials PR and a number, a note appended by the Germans, and which would still have been there when he bought the paintings. And he handed over several canvases without asking for either proof or photographs!"[6] In the end, Fabiani returned twenty-four artworks without a word of protest.

Regarding Paul Pétridès, who died in 1993 at the age of ninety-two, the same 2008 exhibition said that he had been sentenced to three years in prison in 1979 but was freed at seventy-eight because of old age. His claims, after the liberation, that he knew nothing about this illegal trade and that like his colleagues, he had not knowingly bought a single canvas stolen from a Jew, left my grandfather cold: "It is not customary in the trade to buy canvases without first investigating their origins, and to be satisfied with the explanations of German intermediaries unknown to the Paris market."[7]

In the end my grandfather did not bring a case against either Pétridès or Fabiani. So why did he instead decide to pursue unscrupulous Swiss dealers, and why was he more lenient toward the French dealers when some of his paintings were recovered? Was it because he feared that political networks favored those dealers who had collaborated, as they did many civil servants who had been even more seriously compromised? Or because he suspected that the entire art market would be discredited if the public were told about dealers who had behaved badly? Or because he preferred to force them to return his property in his presence and to recover his paintings one by one, in a kind of Count of Monte Cristo–style personal vendetta?

Another paradox that makes me uneasy: my grandfather treated the petty thieves with even greater severity than he did the major crooks, suing them for fraud, abuse of trust, theft, or embezzlement. This was the case with M. Picard, the concierge at 21 rue La Boétie, who had worked there since 1931.

Picard had stolen some objects with the intention— he said in a 1945 statement he prepared for the trial—of safeguarding them before ultimately returning them to the Rosenberg family. "One day," Picard testified, "I was instructed not to let anybody into the house that had been sequestrated by the Germans. On April 25, 1941, the Gestapo moved into the building and I had to give all the keys to the Germans. Two days later they moved out M. Rosenberg's library. On May 2 they moved the furnishings into German cars and replaced them with office materials.* On June 28, I was ordered to leave the premises. In the meantime, I had managed to take various objects from the apartment and the Galerie Rosenberg with the intention of giving it back and only with a view to saving them. It was never my intention to take anything at all for myself."[8]

The testimony of Marguerite Blanchot, the Rosenbergs' housekeeper since the 1920s, is categorical about the building's concierge. "I had the keys to number 21, and Monsieur Rosenberg had told me to move into his apartment. But M. Picard advised me against it and even added that it would be unwise to keep the keys. So I returned them to M. Picard and I came every day until November 1940 to wrap up the linen and the silverware with M. and Mme Picard. It was he who sealed the cases that we filled, and he refused to do it in my presence in spite of my requests. I went back to rue La Boétie several times, but the Picards refused to let me in. The concierge at 20 bis can testify to that. The day before the building was occupied by the Germans, I went to the apartment. When I wanted to get the furniture out, the concierges wouldn't let me."

---

*For the Institute for the Study of Jewish Questions, see the chapter "Number 21 Under the Germans" (p. 27).

René Duval, who worked at the office in the Galerie Rosenberg, testified that he too tried to save some of the belongings from rue La Boétie but that the Picards were opposed. "I never saw anyone taking anything, but I noticed a number of gaps among the paintings, some of which were hung on the walls at the homes of the concierges who told me they had only put them there to save them."

—

Léa Roisneau had been Paul's secretary since 1936. It was she who first alerted him to the looting. In March 1941 she sent my grandfather a letter, saying, "There's nothing left, nothing, nothing, nothing." Her former boss, three thousand miles away in New York, was unaware of so many things. He had no idea that the looting was orchestrated at the highest level of the Nazi hierarchy and that the raids were being carried out against "all the enemies of the Reich" in the occupied territories.

Roisneau also went several times to rue La Boétie, to try to rescue the objects that struck her as most important: the library and the photographs of the paintings. She too observed that the Picards not only took refuge behind the Germans but were further distinguished by their ill will. "One day he—Picard—told me that he wasn't going to let me back into the building, and added that if the Jew Rosenberg came back, he would throw him out the door," said Roisneau in the records.

In fact, Picard had stored objects everywhere: with neighbors, with his relatives. He had even taken Rodin's *Thinker* to an expert, along with a big wood-and-bronze clock. Initially he said he had given my grandfather's youngest brother, Edmond, everything that belonged to Paul; then he confessed that he had lied. Edmond began the inventory of looted objects after the liberation and before Paul returned to France. Mme Picard confirmed: "My husband didn't tell the truth. And after the exodus, we took different things out of M. Rosenberg's house and stored them at the furniture depository: bronzes, a marble bust, an inlaid side table. Also between 140 and 150 bottles of fine wine and champagne (we consumed about fifty of those bottles), and a portrait drawing of Mme Rosenberg."[9]

Pathetic, petty larcenies! Picard had his curtains cut from my grandfather's tapestries and confessed that the Regency barometer mentioned by his wife was actually found in a furniture depository stored in his name. But was my grandfather really more appalled by this than he was by the crimes of the collaborationist art dealers?

The rest—the antique tables, the mahogany chests of drawers, the buffet tables, the chairs—was sold by Captain Sézille, the secretary-general of the IEQJ, to his own employees or used at the Palais Berlitz to furnish the notorious IEQJ exhibition *The Jew and France*.

—

In Floirac the scenario was almost identical: enter, in order of appearance, the occupying forces and the innocent bystanders who, by their own accounts, only wanted to help the family but who ended up taking advantage of the situation.

On September 15, 1940, the Germans arrive at Le

Castel de Floirac at dawn; five vehicles filled with German soldiers and policemen stop outside the house.

The Germans demand to see Louis Le Gall, Paul's chauffeur, who has unsuccessfully been trying for days to persuade the hauler Lamarthonie to send the paintings that have remained in Floirac to Lisbon: some Monet water lilies, a Delacroix, some works by Picasso, Léger, Matisse, Sisley, Vuillard, and Utrillo. In a letter of July 6, 1940, three weeks after his hasty departure from Floirac, Paul has asked Louis for an inventory of all the objects he wants dispatched, including the seventy-five paintings stored at Le Castel. "Don't forget the ones that were left in the chest above the garage, and please be kind enough to check that none is missing," writes my grandfather.

The Germans are well informed and already know everything about Louis. "I was stunned by the amount of information they had about me," Louis later said. Lamarthonie, the trucking company based at 17 cours du Chapeau-rouge in Bordeaux, was to accept delivery of the trunks and crates. It never did so, however, instead requesting the list of objects twice, also asking for the number of paintings. "Then Lamarthonie told me the border was closed. The attitude of M. Lamarthonie and M. and Mme Ledoux toward the 'Israelites' led me to think it unlikely that they were strangers to the information [that the Germans had about me]," Louis Le Gall would testify.[10]

—

The German police search the house from top to bottom and take everything they find to the German Embassy in

Paris, before it is transferred to the Jeu de Paume and then dispersed around Germany and Switzerland, or in France.

A certain Comte de Lestang and someone by the name of Yves Perdoux, probably an obscure art dealer, had apparently made a pact with the Nazis: they would tell them the two addresses in the department of Gironde, that of the house in Floirac and that of the vault in Libourne, where Paul had stored his paintings. In return for this spectacular bounty, they asked for 10 percent of the value of the collection. They tried several times to negotiate their price before finally supplying the Libourne address. In the end, they accepted three Pissarros and a Renoir, far beyond their wildest dreams. But even if you're an informer, do you really negotiate with Nazis?

—

What was the actual conduct of M. and Mme Ledoux? It was probably not very different from that of many people who witnessed the looting, who were powerless but often indifferent and sometimes opportunistic. The postwar trials were not categorical about whether M. and Mme Ledoux did or did not take part in the embezzlements; the Germans weren't given to sharing the fruits of their plunder. But it's more than likely that they did take advantage, even if only by preventing Louis Le Gall from removing the crates that could have been saved.

Later, when objects were found hidden under a woodpile in the garden shed, Mme Ledoux revised her initial statements: "Contrary to what I claimed before, I was in fact able to salvage a painting by Renoir, another by

Degas, a case of silverware, a case of books. My intention was to keep them from the Germans. I planned to return them to M. Rosenberg as soon as possible."[11]

The Germans occupied the property in Floirac until August 27, 1944, when Bordeaux was liberated. M. Ledoux was detained for a time at the camp of Mérignac because of his behavior during the occupation, and then M. and Mme Ledoux regained their property, which they enlarged during the 1950s and ultimately sold to the municipality. That was the same Le Castel to which I paid my emotional visit, seventy years later.

As for Lamarthonie, the hauler, he declared: "I was not aware of any request for transportation being made to me in 1940 by a M. Rosenberg or any of his representatives. However, it is possible that such a request was received by my authorized representative, now deceased, but I can find no trace of this matter in my archives . . ."[12]

The BNCI vault in Libourne, in which my grandfather had imagined his paintings would be safe, was broken into on April 28, 1941, at the request of and in the presence of the occupying authorities. Everything was transferred to a second safe, and this time, on September 5, 1941, a German ERR officer removed the 162 paintings from the BNCI vault. The works were immediately dispatched to Paris, where they fell into Göring's clutches. They were major paintings: Degas, Manet, Bonnard, Matisse, Braque, Picasso, Ingres, Corot, van Gogh, Cézanne, Renoir, Gauguin.

Some of these paintings from Libourne found their way to Parisian dealers. Others found takers in Switzerland

and were recovered after several suits brought by Paul against certain Swiss dealers who demonstrated a remarkable lack of curiosity regarding the provenance of the works they were selling. After all, the backs of many of the canvases that passed through their hands in those years bore labels put there by the ERR meticulously identifying the collections from which they came.

—

"No case," Lynn Nicholas writes, "illustrates these difficulties better than the decades-long struggle of Paul Rosenberg and his heirs, whose possessions reposed not only in France and Germany but also in the neutral country of Switzerland."[13]

Ironically, the most delicate battle of all was fought on Swiss soil.

In September 1945, Nicholas relates, Paul arrived in Zurich armed with lists as well as photographs of paintings that belonged to him. He went straight to the dealers, one after the other. "The dealer Theodor Fischer, in Lucerne, acquired numerous paintings belonging to Paul Rosenberg in Germany, and sold them to private individuals. Paul Rosenberg at last discovered this and launched an action against the Federal Tribunal of Switzerland. The claim was granted, and the defendants were condemned to restore to the plaintiff the paintings demanded from each of them."[14] It was then up to them to make their own claims against the Germans!

Paul's complaints referenced thirty-seven paintings, twenty-two of which were in Fischer's possession. It is easier for me to understand his determination in this case than it is to grasp the impulse that led him to bring suit against small-scale profiteers.

Paul discovered one of his paintings by Matisse, *Woman in a Yellow Armchair*, at the Neupert Gallery in Zurich, where he was even told it was from a private collection. Going higher up the chain, he went to see Emil Bührle, another dealer, "who was surprised to see me, because he had chosen to believe the rumor that I was dead," as Paul told the story. Paul then accused him of knowingly buying stolen goods. Bührle replied that he would return them to Fischer if he got his money back. The two dealers tried to bargain with Paul: he could take back 80 percent of his paintings, leaving the rest. "But Rosenberg was on a crusade and wanted an official, government-to-government settlement," believing that the Swiss government would be willing to negotiate at any price, in order to avoid a scandal.[15]

If my grandfather had to wait for the liberation to find out the extent of the dispersal of his art, as early as 1942 he had been concerned about the fate of stolen paintings all across Europe. He saw it as an attack on the artistic legacy of the war-torn continent. Trying to motivate the Allies, he offered his assistance and cooperation to the profession as a whole, pro bono.

Paul was resolved to return to Paris, to hunt down his scattered collection since 1944, but the War Ministry had not yet authorized French citizens to come back to their country.

As soon as he was able to make contact with the painters closest to him, he asked them for certificates, as he did in this telegram to Matisse in November 1944: "Do you have pictures of last paintings I bought from you, because all taken by Boches [Germans] and resold."

He also insisted, as he did with Braque and Picasso, that Matisse provide a statement that when he visited Floirac in May 1940, he saw one or the other of his own paintings on the walls, proof that Paul had not had sufficient time to sell them before his hasty departure.

—

It was up to the countries in which these acts of plunder had taken place to decide who rightfully owned the recovered works. In France, this task fell to the Commission de Récupération Artistique (CRA, the French Restitution Commission), which was set up in 1944 under the tutelage of Jacques Jaujard, the director of the National Museums of France under the occupation, and of the intrepid Rose Valland.

The CRA quickly returned the works recovered on the Aulnay train, and these were followed by others found at Neuschwanstein Castle in Bavaria. As an expression of gratitude, Paul donated thirty-three of these paintings to major French museums, including the Louvre.

Even today there are works stamped "MNR" and found by the Allies but whose owners have never been identified. And I dare to say it: lying in the basements of prestigious French museums there are still unidentified paintings, whose owners disappeared into the camps and whose inheritors may one day be traced after a vetting of the archives. The museums make no secret of this. They are awaiting the return of those who will not come back.

—

All those battles waged in Paris (whether against big fish or small) or in Switzerland revitalized Paul after long years of waiting. They made him feel that he was achieving a measure of personal justice. At the same time he was gaining perspective. He was clearly aware that these battles were trivial compared with the catastrophe of the Shoah, the atrocities of which were just coming to light. In April 1945 he writes: "We recovered some paintings looted by the Germans, or by dishonest Frenchmen. But I am not going to complain, it's as nothing when you look at the horrors that the Nazis inflicted on human beings of all races, creeds, and colors."

Like the other dealers whose collections had been plundered, he applied for reparations from the Federal Republic of Germany, which in July 1957 passed a law providing financial restitution for losses caused by spoliation. Two years later, in 1959, the Germans proposed a settlement of less than half the sum Paul had claimed. He had died by then, and my grandmother, my uncle, and my mother, wearied by all the procedures involved, accepted their offer.

In 1970, and again in 1980, restitution was back on the agenda, and my mother and my aunt reclaimed paintings by Monet and Léger. Alexandre went so far as to buy back a Degas from its illicit owners. "I do not like so enriching the successors to thieves," he said, as Lynn Nicholas records, "but have come to learn that the defence of one's own and one's family interests is somewhat like politics and indeed life itself. It is principally the art of the possible."[16]

My grandfather's battle to recover his assets, which occupied the latter years of his life, was certainly legitimate, but I can see how it might have been perceived as unseemly by families whose relatives' ashes are forever buried beneath the crematoriums at Auschwitz or even to those who survived the camps. My grandfather was safe, and so was his family. His son had come back a hero of the Second Armored Division, and he still had enough paintings to do business and live well.

Without wishing to play psychologist, I think he needed to make the thieves pay, to do his part in the work of remembrance and of bringing the truth to light. Perhaps he had adopted the phrase that the French Jesuit and scholar Michel de Certeau applied to his historical research, and that was quoted by Annette Wieviorka in the conclusion to her work for the Matteoli Commission, as his credo: "a burial of the dead, that they may return less sadly to their graves."

EPILOGUE

When I began my research, I didn't set out to write a biography. Rather, I wanted to create an homage to my grandfather, a series of impressionist strokes to evoke a man who was a stranger to me yesterday, yet who today seems quite familiar. I wanted to conjure a world, the world of modern painting, one that was mysteriously restored to me, in a random sequence of opened cardboard boxes, and was a product of the French national obsession with security that manifested itself as a bureaucratic aberration.

Yes, this improvised portrait is about a forgotten era, that of France in its greatest glory, the expression of a resplendent artistic culture in the early years of the twentieth century.

About the mutilations of the "world of yesterday"—to quote the title of Stefan Zweig's moving autobiography—which disemboweled Europe, tested the planet, and shattered millions of lives.

About a family that is mine, which I might at last describe—if I allow myself to borrow from Jean-Paul

Sartre—as a whole family, composed of all families and "as good as all of them and no better than any." But a family dearer to me than I would have believed and to which I owe more than I could have imagined.

—

In May 2011, under painful circumstances, I found myself forced once more to live in New York, a prisoner, to some extent, of America. The city of New York itself, which seemed enchanted to me in my childhood, had now become, for both me and my family, a place synonymous with violence and injustice. I had trouble regaining the pleasure of wandering along its streets.

I went back, of course, to Fifty-seventh Street, to the stretch of pavement once occupied by the first Galerie Rosenberg, where the luxury boutiques now extend, between Fifth and Madison. I walked along Seventy-ninth Street, in front of the last of the family galleries, on the Upper East Side, which now strikes me as prodigiously ordinary.

In midtown, I sauntered through the Museum of Modern Art, where, in the room reserved for the impressionists, so rich in dazzling works, I fix my attention on the portrait that stares pointedly at the visitors: that of van Gogh's friend and model Joseph Roulin, the famous postman with the bushy beard, the word "Postes" proudly emblazoned on his cap. That painting was given to the museum by my grandparents, who were so grateful to Alfred Barr and his country for offering them asylum and the recovery of their dignity. How could I allow the chaos of my recent reality to trample cherished childhood memories? How could I resent the entire city over one grueling experience? I never expected these pages, which opened with an identity denied in France, to finish on a forced, turbulent stay in America.

But that of course is another story. If I were a journalist, I might one day write a book about it.

NOTES

RUE LA BOÉTIE
1. E. Tériade, "Feuilles volantes," supplement, *Cahiers d'art* 10 (1927).
2. Quoted in Pierre Nahon, *Les Marchands d'art en France, XIXe et XXe siècles* (Paris: Éditions de la Différence, 1998).

NUMBER 21 UNDER THE GERMANS
1. Quoted in Neil Levi, " 'Judge for Yourselves!': The 'Degenerate Art' Exhibition as Political Spectacle," *October* 85 (Summer 1998): 41–64.
2. Ibid.
3. Lynn H. Nicholas, *The Rape of Europa: The Fate of Europe's Treasures in the Third Reich and the Second World War* (New York: Alfred A. Knopf, 1994).
4. See the historical and intellectual treatment of this passage in ibid.
5. Ibid., 13.
6. Ibid., 7.
7. Laurence Bertrand Dorléac, *L'Art de la défaite, 1940–1944* (Paris: Seuil, 1993).
8. Ibid.
9. Rose Valland, *Le Front de l'art: Défense des collections françaises, 1939–1945* (Paris: Plan, 1961; repr. Paris: Réunion des Musées Nationaux, 1997).
10. Laurent Joly, *Vichy dans la "solution finale": Histoire du Commissariat général aux questions juives, 1941–1944* (Paris: Grasset, 2006).
11. Ibid.

12. Joseph Billig, *Le Commissariat général aux questions juives, 1941–1944* (Vichy: Éditions du Centre, 1955).
13. Quoted in Dorléac, *L'Art de la défaite*.
14. Ibid.
15. Louis-Ferdinand Céline, *Lettres*, edited by Henri Godard and Jean-Paul Louis (Paris: Gallimard, 2009).

FLOIRAC

1. Correspondence quoted by Alex Danchev, Braque's authorized biographer, in *Georges Braque: A Life* (New York: Arcade Publishing, 2005).
2. Ibid.
3. Document quoted in the lawyers' notes for recuperations after the war. Family archives.
4. Henri Matisse archives.
5. Ibid.
6. Paul Rosenberg, "French Artists and the War," *Art in Australia*, December 1941–January 1942.
7. Emmanuelle Loyer, *Paris à New York: Intellectuels et artistes français en exil 1940–1947* (Paris: Grasset, 2005).
8. Quoted in ibid.
9. See Dan Franck, *Minuit* (Paris: Grasset, 2010).
10. Family archives.
11. Loyer, *Paris à New York*.

GENNEVILLIERS

1. Loyer, *Paris à New York*.

DEALER

1. Pierre Assouline, *L'Homme de l'art: D.-H. Kahnweiler, 1884–1979* (Paris: Gallimard Folio, 1989).
2. Ibid.
3. Ibid.
4. Michael C. FitzGerald, *Making Modernism: Picasso and the Creation of the Market for Twentieth-Century Art* (Berkeley: University of California Press, 1996).

5. Family archives.
6. Assouline, *L'Homme de l'art.*
7. Rosenberg, "French Artists and the War."
8. Albert Wolff, "Le Calendrier parisien," *Le Figaro*, April 3, 1876.
9. Family archives.

CHÂTEAUDUN, OPÉRA, AND MADISON AVENUE

1. Paul Rosenberg: "*Je suis né . . .* ," autobiographical sketch, from which the quotations in this chapter are taken. Family archives.
2. Tériade, "Feuilles volantes."
3. Henri Matisse archives.
4. Ibid.
5. Nahon, *Les Marchands d'art.*
6. Hector Feliciano, *The Lost Museum: The Nazi Conspiracy to Steal the World's Greatest Works of Art* (New York: Basic Books, 1997).
7. René Gimpel, *Journal d'un collectionneur: Marchand de tableaux* (Paris: Calmann-Lévy, 1963).
8. *The New York Times*, December 7, 1953.
9. Family archives.
10. Ibid.
11. Henri Matisse archives.
12. Ibid.

MOTHER AND CHILD

1. Picasso archives, Musée Picasso.
2. FitzGerald, *Making Modernism.*

PAUL AND PIC

1. The language is from FitzGerald, *Making Modernism.*
2. Nahon, *Les Marchands d'art.*
3. Ibid.
4. FitzGerald, *Making Modernism.*
5. Family archives.
6. Roland Penrose, *Picasso: His Life and Work*, 3rd ed. (Berkeley: University of California Press, 1981).

7. All the letters that follow in this chapter are from the Picasso archives.
8. FitzGerald, *Making Modernism.*
9. Pierre Daix, *Dictionnaire Picasso* (Paris : Robert Laffont, 1995).

BOULEVARD MAGENTA
1. Vincent Noce, "L'Histoire contre Wildenstein," *Libération*, May 13, 2000.

A LONG RELATIONSHIP
1. Henri Matisse archives.

THE WAR YEARS IN NEW YORK
1. Henri Matisse archives.
2. Ibid.
3. Franck, *Minuit.*
4. Loyer, *Paris à New York.*

PREOCCUPATIONS OF THE HEART
1. Dorléac, *L'Art de la défaite.*
2. Danchev, *Georges Braque.*
3. Ibid.
4. Ibid.
5. Franck, *Minuit.*
6. Rosenberg, "French Artists and the War."
7. Ibid.
8. Maurice de Vlaminck, "Opinions libres . . . sur la peinture," *Comœdia*, June 6, 1942.
9. Dorléac, *L'Art de la défaite.*
10. In his book *Le Cabinet des douze*, Laurent Fabius mentions this canvas, as well as *The Charnel House* of 1945, showing how during this period Picasso's clashing, violent, broken painting symbolizes the trauma of war.
11. Picasso archives.
12. Dorléac, *L'Art de la défaite.*
13. Franck, *Minuit.*

14. Dorléac, *L'Art de la défaite*.
15. Rosenberg, "French Artists and the War."
16. "Picasso" file, document requesting naturalization, November 30, 1942, Archives of the Paris Police Prefecture.

THE TRAIN, SCHENKER, AND THE ART OF THE POSSIBLE

1. Valland, *Le Front de l'art*.
2. Ibid.
3. "Le pillage de l'art en France pendant l'Occupation et la situation des 2,000 œuvres confiées aux musées nationaux" (The Looting of Art in France During the French Occupation and the Location of the 2,000 Works Confiscated from the National Museums), a contribution from the administration of the Musées de France and the Centre Pompidou to the works of the Matteoli Commission on the spoliation of Jews in France, 2000.
4. Annette Wieviorka, "Des spoliations aux restitutions," in Tal Bruttmann (ed.), *Persécutions et spoliations des Juifs pendant la seconde guerre mondiale* (Grenoble: Presses Universitaires de Grenoble, 2004), 13–22.
5. Records of the Office of Strategic Services (RG 226); formerly Security Classified Intelligence reports ("XL" Series), 1941–1946. Document in English and French. For the latter, the list is signed "Michel Martin, chargé de mission au Département des peintures, rue de Tocqueville, November 7, 1944."
6. Family archives.
7. Ibid.
8. Trial record, family archives.
9. Ibid.
10. Ibid.
11. Ibid.
12. Ibid.
13. Nicholas, *Rape of Europa*, 415.
14. *Journal des tribunaux*, Geneva, August 1948.
15. Nicholas, *Rape of Europa*, 418.
16. Ibid., 421.

BIBLIOGRAPHY

Assouline, Pierre. *Le Dernier des Camondo*. Revised and expanded edition. Paris: Gallimard Folio, 1999.

———. *L'Homme de l'art: D.-H. Kahnweiler, 1884–1979*. Paris: Gallimard Folio, 1989.

Billig, Joseph. *Le Commissariat général aux questions juives, 1941–1944*. 3 Volumes. Vichy: Éditions du Centre, 1955.

Cabanne, Pierre. *Le Siècle de Picasso*. 4 volumes. Revised and expanded edition. Paris: Gallimard Folio-Essais, 1992.

Céline, Louis-Ferdinand. *Lettres*. Edited by Henri Godard and Jean-Paul Louis. Paris: Gallimard, 2009.

Daix, Pierre. *Dictionnaire Picasso*. Paris: Robert Laffont, 1995.

Danchev, Alex. *Georges Braque: A Life*. New York: Arcade Publishing, 2005.

Desprairies, Cécile. *Paris dans la Collaboration*. Paris: Seuil, 2009.

———. *Ville lumière, années noires: Les Lieux du Paris de la Collaboration*. Paris: Denoël, 2008.

de Staël, Françoise. *Nicolas de Staël: Catalogue raisonné de l'œuvre peint*. Neuchâtel, Switzerland: Ides et Calendes, 1997.

de Vlaminck, Maurice. "Opinions libres . . . sur la peinture." *Comœdia*, June 6, 1942.

Dorléac, Laurence Bertrand. *L'Art de la défaite, 1940–1944*. Paris: Seuil, 1993.

Duncan, David Douglas. *Goodbye Picasso*. New York: Grosset & Dunlap, 1974.

Fabius, Laurent. *Le Cabinet des douze: Regards sur des tableaux qui font la France*. Paris: Gallimard, 2010.

Feliciano, Hector. *The Lost Museum: The Nazi Conspiracy to Steal the World's Greatest Works of Art*. New York: Basic Books, 1997.

FitzGerald, Michael C. *Making Modernism: Picasso and the Creation of the Market for Twentieth-Century Art.* Berkeley: University of California Press, 1996.

Franck, Dan. *Minuit.* Paris: Grasset, 2010.

Gee, Malcolm. *Dealers, Critics, and Collections of Modern Painting: Aspects of the Parisian Art Market Between 1910 and 1930.* New York: Garland Publishing, 1981.

Gimpel, René. *Journal d'un collectionneur: Marchand de tableaux.* Paris: Calmann-Lévy, 1963.

Green, Christopher. *Cubism and Its Enemies: Modern Movements and Reaction in French Art, 1916–1928.* New Haven, CT: Yale University Press, 1987.

Joly, Laurent. *Vichy dans la "solution finale": Histoire du Commissariat général aux questions juives, 1941–1944.* Paris: Grasset, 2006.

Levi, Neil. "'Judge for Yourselves!': The 'Degenerate Art' Exhibition as Political Spectacle," *October* 85 (Summer 1998): 41–64.

Loyer, Emmanuelle. *Paris à New York: Intellectuels et artistes français en exil 1940–1947.* Paris: Grasset, 2005.

Nahon, Pierre. *Les Marchands d'art en France, XIXe et XXe siècles.* Paris: Éditions de la Différence, 1998.

Nicholas, Lynn H. *The Rape of Europa: The Fate of Europe's Treasures in the Third Reich and the Second World War.* New York: Alfred A. Knopf, 1994.

Noce, Vincent. "L'Histoire contre Wildenstein." *Libération*, May 13, 2000.

Penrose, Roland. *Picasso: His Life and Work.* 3rd edition. Berkeley: University of California Press, 1981.

Rosenberg, Paul. "French Artists and the War." *Art in Australia*, December 1941–January 1942.

Tériade, E. "Feuilles volantes," supplement, *Cahiers d'art* 10 (1927).

Valland, Rose. *Le Front de l'art: Défense des collections françaises, 1939–1945.* Paris: Plon, 1961; reprint edition, Paris: Réunion des Musées Nationaux, 1997.

Vollard, Ambroise. *En écoutant Cézanne, Degas, Renoir.* Paris: Grasset, 2003.

Wieviorka, Annette. "Des spoliations aux restitutions." In *Persécutions et spoliations des Juifs pendant la seconde guerre mondiale*, edited by Tal Bruttmann, 13–22. Grenoble: Presses Universitaires de Grenoble, 2004.

Wolff, Albert. "Le Calendrier parisien." *Le Figaro*, April 3, 1876.

ACKNOWLEDGMENTS

All the letters and quotations from Paul Rosenberg cited in this book are previously unpublished. Most of them come from my personal archives, as well as those kept by my aunt Elaine Rosenberg. I should particularly like to thank her, as well as my cousin Elisabeth Rosenberg-Clark, for graciously granting me access to the many boxes of documents from my grandfather's gallery, from before and after the war. These archives were preserved in New York, at my aunt's house, before being passed on to the Museum of Modern Art.

Thanks, of course, to Anne Baldassari, the director of the Musée Picasso, who, before the construction that forced the museum to close for more than two years, granted me shelter in its library so that I could dig around in the ample collection of letters from Paul Rosenberg to Pablo Picasso, which were given to the museum by the Picasso family. She generously and enthusiastically allowed me to reproduce extracts from that correspondence here.

ACKNOWLEDGMENTS

Wanda de Guébriant, the director of the Matisse archives that were kept in the painter's house at Issy-les-Moulineaux, helped me access the archives of Henri Matisse and allowed me to reproduce some of the painter's correspondence with my grandfather, again previously unpublished. I am extremely grateful to her.

Finally, I should like to mention Didier Schulmann, the curator at the Musée National d'Art Moderne, Centre Pompidou, who was so kind as to grant me access to the photographic documents of the exhibitions at the Galerie Paul Rosenberg and to allow me to reproduce them.

ILLUSTRATION CREDITS

Frontispiece: Private collection/Succession Picasso, 2012

A NOTE ABOUT THE AUTHOR

Anne Sinclair is Paul Rosenberg's granddaughter and one of France's best-known journalists. For thirteen years she was the host of *7 sur 7*, a weekly news and politics television show for which she interviewed world figures of the day, including Bill Clinton, Mikhail Gorbachev, and Madonna. The editorial director of *Le Huffington Post* (France), Sinclair has written two bestselling books on politics.